What Others Are Saying About
THE FOOD IS A LIE:
THE TRUTH IS WITHIN...

"The best thing about Bronwyn's book is that it's practical and gives real-life strategies to overcome real-life challenges to living peacefully in your own skin. If you are ready to love yourself in the body you have, Bronwyn will show you how in this fabulous and practical book."

Sonia Choquette
Author of Trust Your Vibes

"With practice and awareness all things are possible and Bronwyn has shown this with her life. Thank you for sharing your dream with many and may we all walk in life, in love with everything we create."

Don Jose Luis Ruiz
Toltec Wisdom Guide

"So positive, so vulnerable, so truthful, and so practically helpful! You do not have to be overweight to immensely profit from Bronwyn's book. I would sincerely recommend it to any of us because it is about life, attitude, faith, and our relationship to the material world. This is actually very solid spirituality – without even pretending to be!"

Richard Rohr, O.F.M.
Center for Action and Contemplation
Albuquerque, New Mexico

THE FOOD IS A LIE:
THE TRUTH IS WITHIN

A Spiritual Solution to

Weight Loss and Balanced Health

Dear Mary

Abundant blessings

along your journey

with love,

Bronwyn

THE FOOD IS A LIE:
THE TRUTH IS WITHIN

A Spiritual Solution to

Weight Loss and Balanced Health

BRONWYN MARMO

TRIPLE B PUBLISHING

Dedication

This book is dedicated to all those

who are searching for peace with food,

weight, body image and self-esteem.

May you find your innermost

truth,

strength,

inspiration,

and love.

Table of Contents

part in helping me make sense of my spirituality and balanced health: Fr. Richard Rohr, who reminded me to "Be still, and know", Pat Julian, Martha Chaffee, Jayne Jewell, Eleanor Gross, Jim Springer, Lou and Bonnie Cornille, and Betty Bova, who taught me the power and beauty of saying "Yes".

A big thank you goes to my literary agents Michael Ebeling and Ana Hays for their contribution in helping launch this message of balanced health out into the world. I also appreciate the wisdom and talents of J.J. Smith-Moore of Sibling Press, who helped bring this book to life with her artistry, color and style.

I'm filled with gratitude to all those who were open to reading the manuscript as it was in development, offering their support, critique and editing expertise, including Karen Van Allen, Lisa Simkins, Linda Simpson, Mary Silliman, Marilyn Pritchard, Angel McCormick, Shannon O'Brien, Sasha Ginsburg, George and Jan Fenimore and Mary Kay Mueller.

In deep love and appreciation, I would like to thank all those who participated in the workshops, seminars and retreats that I conducted over the last few years, as well as, to my personal coaching clients. Their courage and willingness to embrace their inner journey to balanced health is awe-inspiring. I learned and received as much from them, as they did from me. Without them, this book would not have come into existence.

Finally, to the loving God that was present during the writing of this book, thank You for the grace to hear Your "voice" and the willingness to put what I heard into action.

be reading in communion with the Spirit. This invitation to the Divine awakens your heart and soul, allowing the possibility of extracting the nectar that is present on these pages. An example of just some of the fruits that may come, include opening yourself up to hearing a voice beyond your own knowing, seeing sparkles of beauty in places you never noticed before, and passionately and deeply falling in love with this world and everyone in it, including yourself.

in her surrender. As she shared her own inner struggle with the revisions, especially the third, and what I thought would be the last one, her description confirmed she also felt the surrender. This portion of her journey, and my role in it, felt complete.

To my surprise, Bronwyn contacted me after some months to say the book was revised again and she would like my feedback. I experienced the fourth revision as really a deepening and refining of the transformation that was reflected in the third revision. She had integrated the understanding, insights, and her connection with the Divine. This was apparent on a deeper level in her personal life, her relationships, and her writing. This fourth revision was really all Bronwyn and the Divine, an authentic claiming of her experience in her words, images, and style. She came full circle and arrived "home".

In the following pages you have the opportunity to share in Bronwyn's journey and the wisdom she earned. There are personal stories, practical strategies, and heart-felt encouragement from a woman who has "been there". The book is, among other things, an invitation to encounter that same connection with the "something more" that really has no name. It is an invitation to find a reliable guide, a sense of what honors you, a knowing of right relationship. Bronwyn invites and encourages you to enter more deeply into an authentic relationship with the Truth as it speaks within your heart. Through this relationship, you will discover right relationship

PART ONE

"Let there be no seeing, no hearing;
enfold the spirit in quietude
and the body will right itself."

- Chuang Tzu

Introduction

*"With your focus you create your life,
your world and everything in it"*
- Baba Hari Dass

My story begins in May of 1997, at a time when the light inside me was quickly dimming and my life was spiraling out of control. I was emotionally, physically and spiritually debilitated because food was ruling my life. For years, I had been waking up in the morning feeling defeated. Like alcoholics or drug addicts who are obsessed with finding their next "fix", my first thoughts in the morning were, "What can I eat?" And, "Where can I get it?" Then, in fear and despair I would think to myself, "Oh no, another day". I would let out a big sigh and pull the covers over my head to hide. I desperately wanted to fade away, to silently slide into nothingness. I felt as though the weight of the world was on my shoulders and I didn't want to go on anymore.

At 5' 3", I wore a size 16 and was considered obese, weighing in at 173 pounds. I had struggled with my weight since childhood. I felt different and separate from other people, not knowing where I belonged. I turned to food to comfort and soothe me, as if it was my best friend and lover. I used food as a coping mechanism to escape the emptiness I healing the whole self through an innermost source of love, which defies all description and surpasses all knowledge, yet is made known to each one of us in a profound, personal and intimate way. This supernatural force, perfect, omnipotent and omniscient, is within you and around you at all times; readily available to aid you with every problem, question and conflict that may arise. Nothing is too great or too small, including your health challenges.

After desperately trying to look thin, spending decades on the deprivation and binge roller coaster, trying many weight-loss diet centers, liquid diets and fasts, I finally figured out that dieting was a temporary band-aid, hiding issues I hadn't dealt with. I came to see that I had to stop looking for answers outside of myself. I needed to look within.

The solution to permanent weight loss and balanced health is not found in the $40 billion a year diet industry. It is discovered when we reflect inward to our innermost source of truth and wisdom. It's not something that is known in the mind, but in the soul, when we leave our obsession with the body behind and go to the body's vital source.

"We are searching in the wrong place.
The answer is beyond you… beyond me… beyond self.
Let's go where the answer is."
- Carl Jung

This book is designed to help you unlock the answers that

one, take the time to reflect inward and sit in the moment. Allow it to become a meditation that helps you nurture and cultivate a deeper connection with your one true Source. Quieting your mind and being in tune with love, hope, faith and trust, creates the space for transformation. Prayer is the vehicle that brings great personal strength to tackle any challenge, especially your health issues.

Part I is designed to lay the groundwork for the rest of the book. In it, I will share with you simple and practical methods designed to open you up to hearing your loving, trusting guide within. When you live from your center, you can't help but taste life in a way you've never done before. Foods that once seduced you and compelled you into eating them, no longer have power. Self-defeating thoughts which used to drag you down and beat you up no longer have influence over you. You will never be able to escape the onslaught of advertisements on television, radio, magazines, billboards and the internet that promote chewy and gooey, or crunchy and crispy, high-fat, high-salt foods. They're everywhere. What you will be able to do is change how you respond or react to those ads. You have all the power to choose.

Part II provides simple ways you can empower yourself in your relationship with food. I won't tell you what you should or shouldn't eat or the best formula for nourishing your body. I am still, and will always be, learning because my physical needs continue to change. Plus, you would be robbed of the joy of your own discovery as you go within your

Surely, there are others who are a lot more qualified, such as doctors, nutritionists, or even the "hard bodies" who barely have an ounce of fat. Frankly, if I were to act on *my* will, you'd find me running in the opposite direction, hiding under the covers of my bed with a box of chocolates.

But, faith and courage stir deep inside me, as I am called forth into this great power of love that is always trying to reveal itself. It compels me to walk this path that is laid out before me, in spite of how uncertain I feel. Then, I would think, "Who better to carry this message of balanced health?" I have been on the front-lines in the battle with food, weight, body image and self-esteem for decades. My body bears the truth as stretch marks spread wildly across my hips and belly as if designed by a crazed spider, building its web. Also, years and years of yo-yo dieting have taken their toll, as my sagging skin can testify. Yes, who better to help others who are struggling, than someone who has bought, sold, leased and owned the taxing life of obsession? Yet, now that same person is discovering a new way of life by following unbridled love which breeds truth, compassion and freedom.

Achieving balance in all areas of life is one of the foremost goals of most people. If your life is in balance, you have a better chance of being content, gratified, and to celebrate being alive.

Imagine a video camera sitting on top of a tripod, continually shooting pictures of you. One leg of that tripod represents your emotional life, the second leg is your physical

CHAPTER ONE

My Story

The following thoughts were taken from my personal journal:

From my earliest memories as a child, I felt different and set apart from others. I saw myself as fat while everyone else was skinny. I was haunted by the pain and shame I felt in school as kids would tease me about my weight. Early on, I developed a distorted image of my body as I longed to be thin, so I could fit in with the other kids.

I went on my first diet when I was about 11 years old. I would starve myself for days at a time, and then scavenge through the pantry, eating anything I could get my hands on. That was the beginning of my vicious cycle of deprivation and binge eating.

In my teens, I sought comfort in my best friend and companion – food. One of my favorite loves, was a double-chocolate, Stir N' Frost cake. I would bake the cake in its' cardboard pan, then squeeze the frosting on top, consuming it all emptiness that loomed heavily within.

I had promised myself I was going to be a "skinny bride" and when I met my future husband, I went on another diet losing 30 pounds, slimming down to 120 pounds. With my new thin look, my broadcasting career took off. I was promoted to the nightly news anchor position and developed a steady following of viewers.

Ironically, my wedding day was one of the happiest days of my life, not only because I was in love, but because I was skinny and in total control of my food. Little did I know that moment was fleeting as I was only able to control my cravings just long enough to get through the wedding reception. Then, I ate everything in sight, even the top layer of our wedding cake that we were going to save for our first year anniversary. The beautiful clothes I had just purchased for my honeymoon did not fit when I returned home. I felt totally defeated and hopeless.

I gained 55 pounds my first year of marriage, then found out I was pregnant. My weight continued to rapidly climb, much more than during a typical pregnancy. I loved seeing my belly grow from the child developing inside me, but agonized over the tremendous amount of excess weight that went beyond the baby. Food was controlling my life in an unhealthy cycle of secretive binge eating. I was drowning and clung to food as if it was my life preserver.

I had an insatiable appetite and I would eat in the middle of the night, only to go back to bed and wake up to a hearty breakfast. During my lunch break, I would grab a big meal, a baby with his special needs. I still looked pregnant, but didn't have a baby to show for it. I wallowed in self-pity, allowing the emptiness to take up more space.

There were too many sad memories for my husband and me in Oregon, so we abruptly decided to move. I contacted the television station and informed them I would not be returning from maternity leave. We spent five months traveling to places where nobody knew anything about the baby. I was anonymous and happily removed from the rest of the world that I sought desperately to escape.

It wasn't long before my sadness and despair caught up with me and I sought the only comfort I knew. I was back to eating huge quantities of food, anything to numb my pain. I closed myself off in a dark room with the shades drawn shut, watching television and eating way beyond being full. I felt so helpless because I knew I couldn't stop. I was eating so much that my stomach was swollen and I could barely stand up. It was all I could do to waddle over to the bed and fall into a sugar coma. I didn't leave the house except to go to the store to buy more food. I entertained the idea of putting myself on a liquid diet, but soon talked myself out of it because I couldn't stop eating.

We settled in the Southwest, anxious to start our new lives. As much as I tried, I couldn't run away from my past. I continued to wear maternity clothes for almost a year after I gave birth because that was all that fit me. I felt humiliated and self-conscious but refused to buy new clothes until I lost forced myself to walk over to a wall-mirror that was hanging in an adjacent room. Still holding the box of cookies, I looked at my reflection, yet did not recognize the person in front of me. Tears were streaming down my face as I continued to put more cookies in my mouth. At that moment I knew something was wrong with me because I couldn't stop eating, even if I wanted to. With crumbs stuck to the side of my mouth, I fell down to my knees, reached up and cried out in agony and desperation, "God, help me! Please help me!"

Just then, a deep, loving feeling enveloped my body. It was so beautiful and so passionate I was overcome with emotion and fell onto the floor in amazement and awe. During that moment which seemed to freeze in time, I got a glimpse into how wide and long and high and deep is the unlimited well of love radiating forth from the Source of true life.

The moment may have been a few seconds or a few minutes, I don't know. It was so powerful that if it were any longer, I would have passed out. Never had I felt so alive, so balanced, and so at peace. The flow of limitless energy within me and around me convinced me that I was loved more than I had ever imagined. For the first time in my life, I felt satiated. The emptiness in my soul was filled-up in a way food could never do. I was forever changed on that fateful day, realizing I no longer had to be in control of my food, my weight, my body, or my life.

that is carefully tucked away in a secret box in my soul. But, the more I sought it, the less I found it. The more I pushed it, the less I was pulled into it. The more I tried to figure it out in my mind, the less I felt it in my soul. The more I tried to control it, the more out of control I became. Over time and through many moments of frustration and disillusionment, I finally listened with an open heart.

"Be still, and know that I am God."
- Psalm 46:10

"That's it?" I asked myself in disbelief. "That's all?" It almost seems too easy. "Be still, and know that I am God." I was trying to make it so difficult. I thought I needed to do something, achieve something, control something, even fix something, (namely me), before I could be in the presence of divinity. My initial actions were actually driving me further away from my innermost love. Now I was discovering that I didn't have to "do" anything. I was not being called to be successful or efficient. I was being called to be faithful. I didn't have to exert any force or willpower. I just needed to "be", offering my emptiness, so that my soul could be filled with the spirit of love.

"Work is not always required...
there is such a thing as sacred idleness,
the cultivation of which is now fearfully neglected."
- George MacDonald

37

perfect harmony with the spirit, giving you the fuel to go forth and be a light in the world. They provide the nourishment your body needs to give you the health and vibrancy to live this day to its fullest. They prepare you to be a sharpened tool ready for use at any moment. They satisfy your stomach while your heart and soul are dancing in the spirit. These foods bring you balance and clarity, and as you are eating them, you can smell the fragrance of grace.

CHAPTER TWO

Awaken To Your Silent Voice Within

*"Still your mind in me, still yourself in me,
and without a doubt you shall be united with me,
Lord of Love, dwelling in your heart."*
- Bhagavad Gita

No one can teach you or tell you how to open your mind and your soul. The experience is personal and unique to each individual. I can only hint at it by sharing some of the clues that have helped me to know and hold my center of quietness within. For me, it is a personal and intimate communication that two passionate lovers share and explore. It is not found in the head, but is felt in the heart. It is oneness with the soul; a closeness that transcends thought, surpasses breath, exceeds choice, and goes beyond awareness.

Putting it in more relatable terms, it may be described as the deepest love that you have felt or currently feel for your spouse, lover, parent, child, sibling, close friend or pet. It may me continuously for extended periods of time. Every day, I make it a priority to get in touch with my innermost feelings of love, joy and compassion, as they gently warm and soften up my heart. I hold that relationship in the highest regard like a lover or trusted companion. It helps me stay grounded, focused and rooted in my center of peace.

> *"Interior silence is the perfect seed bed*
> *for divine love to take root…*
> *Divine love has the power to grow and transform us.*
> *The purpose of contemplative prayer is to facilitate*
> *the process of inner transformation."*
> - Thomas Keating

There are different avenues to the indwelling of the Divine through silent prayer, meditation and contemplation. I encourage you to seek out the right method for you. Over the years, I have practiced several different forms and each one was perfect for that particular time in my life. There is no one right way or even a wrong way to do it, yet silence is a key element. Thomas Keating, a Cistercian priest, monk, abbot, and co-founder of the Centering Prayer Movement and of Contemplative Outreach writes in his book, *Invitation to Love*, "Silence is God's first language; everything else is a poor translation. In order to hear that language, we must learn to be still and to rest in God."

A valuable book to help you on your journey is Keating's

Center in that space until you feel relaxed. Thoughts and feelings are more than likely going to spring up into your consciousness. You may also find your imagination drifting off or you may have a certain memory. All of those responses are normal, so don't despair or react in any way. Gently release them without judgment or attachment and continue being drawn back into the silence with your breath.

> *"I am open to the guidance of synchronicity,*
> *and do not let expectations hinder my path."*
> - Dalai Lama

At first, I didn't think anything was happening. "What am I doing?" I asked myself as I tried very hard to sit still. I hadn't realized it was going to take discipline to stay focused on this deep quiet. "The silence is uncomfortable. I want to fill it with noise. I want to create a diversion. I want to scream, so I don't have to hear the blaring sound of silence ---." Tenderly, I am reminded to step aside from my thoughts and expectations and allow my breath to guide me to my center of quiet within. Breathing in, breathing out, slowing down, settling in, sitting quietly in this calm, peaceful space.

Watching your breath allows you to still your mind, yet it will not distract you from getting to your innermost quiet. Don't allow frustration or anxiety to divert you from your practice. There is no wrong way to be in your center, receiving and renewing awareness. Embrace all thoughts and feelings

Reflections On

CHAPTER TWO

(The following reflections are offered to you as meditations that will help you nurture and cultivate a deeper connection with your silent voice within. While sitting quietly and breathing slowly and deeply, place your intention on one reflection at a time. Gently clear away thoughts of judgment and attachment, making room for the full mystery and sacredness of the message to permeate your heart and soul.)

~ I awaken to my silent voice within.

~ I practice opening my mind and soul, knowing the experience is personal and unique to me.

~ My special moment of love lives inside of me and is available at every moment.

~ Creating my life where all things spring from love, allows for transformation in my spiritual, emotional and physical well-being.

~ I gently release all thoughts and feelings, without judgment or attachment, and continue being drawn back into the silence with my breath.

~ When I align myself with my innermost being, I put myself on a path that is life-giving.

doing?" I asked over and over as I found myself doing things to improve my health; things that I could never have imagined doing in the past. I didn't fully understand what I was doing, nor why, but I knew that I had to, even though I was full of doubt and fear. I knew if I didn't adopt these changes, I would be betraying my innermost truth.

"What am I doing?" I asked as I noticed myself eating three meals a day with an afternoon snack. That was a foreign concept to me as I was used to eating anything I wanted, anytime of the day or night. I wanted to fight it. I wanted to doubt. "Maybe I got my signals crossed. Maybe I'm not supposed to eat like this. Maybe this is wrong. It all seems so bizarre. My world seems so different." Despite my confusion, I believed I had to continue on in faith, riding the wave of my innermost consciousness.

"What am I doing?" I asked as I ate fresh vegetables and fruit, whole grains and proteins and was surprised that I was enjoying the taste. I was used to going months without any sort of fresh produce. I wanted to resist. I didn't want to eat healthy foods. I wanted my comfort foods. "I miss the old familiar tastes," I cried to myself as I longed for the foods that allowed me to escape into a hole. But love kept gently nudging me forward. Deep down, I knew I was on the right path.

"What am I doing?" I asked as I walked outside in the fresh air. For my oversized body, taking a walk down the street was a big deal. I wanted to give up. I wanted to refuse. "I don't want to put on my tennis shoes. I don't want to begins. We cannot anticipate lasting change of our old behaviors without faith. With faith comes understanding and awareness, like the light along the darkened hallway. Faith is a firm belief in something that you cannot prove. It's a total trust that is ever-present and available to all. To live in faith means to live in surrender to what is, becoming fully present and open to the moment. Faith means knowing and accepting that you are exactly where you are supposed to be, at this weight, in this moment, right now. Since you can't see the whole picture, I encourage you not to judge yourself based on outer effects. You have been called to be in this experience for a reason; you may or may not ever know why your weight is an issue at this time in your life. Through it all, though, you have this sense that you are on the right track and that you are loved more than you can imagine. Faith means giving thanks for the inward journey that has already begun.

> *"From all this it is evident that faith is not just*
> *one moment of the spiritual life,*
> *not just a step to something else.*
> *It is that acceptance to God which is the very climate*
> *of all spiritual living. It is the beginning of communion."*
> - Thomas Merton

With the absence of faith, we are living in fear. This keeps us paralyzed from moving forward and creating a right relationship with ourselves and with others. Fear to grace. "Yes" to trust. "Yes" to balanced health. "Yes" to healthy food choices. "Yes" to everything that springs forth from God.

Life works this way because the highest and best "Yes" is always being said to you. The choice is yours. You have been given free will to decide whether you will accept this divine "Yes" or choose another path. Living in faith is surrendering to your innermost guide, joining the dynamic energy that created the world and breathing together as one.

CHAPTER FOUR

Make Peace With Your Hungry Side

*"We do not know the weight of this 'self' we
are carrying until we put it down."*
- Zen saying

Within one year of my spiritual experience in 1997, I released more than 50 pounds as I consistently made the choice to say, "Yes" to balanced health. I continued my daily practice of resting in silence, and rooted myself in passionate, unbridled love. I stayed open to wherever I was being led. An infinite power that loved me more than I could imagine was guiding me. By grace, I was able to prayerfully make healthy food choices and develop an exercise regime that I came to enjoy. Each day, I consciously surrendered to my innermost truth and renewed my commitment of willingness.

I continued to practice observing my thoughts and actions throughout my day. When I veered off course paralyzed and unable to move forward.

Through the love and support of my husband, close friends, family members, and counseling, I uncovered one of the causes of my anxiety. When I was a very young girl, I participated in what is called "doctor's play", an innocent sexual exploration between two small kids. What I didn't know at the time though, was that a part of me had judged the activities as inappropriate, dirty, bad and scary. Although I was a willing participant, I realize now that I was too young to make that decision. My body was not mature enough to handle the consequences. The tension manifested in my body. That painful discovery left me feeling confused, shameful, scared and extremely angry.

I felt betrayed by my innermost truth. Not only about my experience as a child, but now the residual conflict that I had to deal with as an adult. The situation shook my foundation and I did not feel peaceful or happy. I began to second-guess myself and didn't think I could trust my instincts anymore. I tried desperately to distance myself from my innermost guide because I blamed myself for causing the pain. Acting out with defiance and anger, I made a conscious decision to live my life according to *my* will. I lashed out like a spoiled child, turning my back on my innermost guide. I would scream, "How could You let me go through this?" The wounds felt so deep that I soon became depressed due to my own emptiness. All of my past hurts came to the forefront as I felt like a victim once again. My fall into the abyss seemed swift, and quickly gained

I was filled with such pain and shame. My ego and pride would not allow me to show anyone how out of control I had become. I hid my food, my thoughts and my feelings.

Over this period of time, my physical body began to break down. I was outwardly showing signs of wear-and-tear from stress. The color in my face turned sallow. I noticed a whole new crop of broken blood vessels around my cheeks and under my eyes. I won't even mention the new wrinkles. Also, my eyes were void of the brightness and shine that were there when I was healthy.

*"God holds back his infinite mercy from rushing
to the rescue when we are in temptation and difficulties...
If the divine help comes too soon before the work of purification
and healing has been accomplished, it may frustrate
our ultimate ability to live the divine life."*
- Thomas Keating

After I was completely honest with myself, I knew I had to release the thoughts I continued to hold about this experience. Once they were brought to the surface so that I could examine them in the light, I realized the little girl was simply curious. She wanted to be loved, just as we all do. By holding her hostage in my mind for her childish behavior, I was continuing to harm her. When I allowed the light to shine forth, I was also reminded of the joy and laughter that I experienced as a fun-loving, precocious child. Realizing that

The journey back to feeling physically healthy, vibrant and energetic began when I came face-to-face with my own shortcomings. It was through humility that I found the strength to make peace with my hungry, ego-based side. It was no longer the part of me that I disdained or denied or beat up or ran away from; but rather it was a part of me that I could embrace, accept and love. Changing my thoughts helped me to rise again in the light of the loving arms of divinity.

I used to desperately pray asking that my food challenges be removed. I wanted them to finally disappear and cease to be an issue in my life. I didn't want to think about food again. Now, I see that in order to have true peace and serenity with food, I also need to be observant and respectful of the discord. It is with the opposing forces (negative and positive - dark and light - hot and cold) that the world keeps spinning and creates Chi - the giving life force.

Your ego-based self and your faith-based self are two sides of the same coin. You can't have one without the other. They are two opposing forces, both are vital and serve their purpose. In order to know one, you must acknowledge the other. If you desire peace in your life, respect turmoil; if you want joy, show consideration for pain; if you long for happiness, embrace sadness. Both sides are used to free us from bondage.

"My business is not to remake myself,
But make the absolute best of what God made."
- Robert Browning

swirling around with my tongue.

In my mind, I had already eaten the double-chocolate cake. The feelings of shame and guilt overcame me. I proceeded to beat myself up saying, "Look at you. You certainly don't need to eat a piece of double-chocolate cake." That thought led into more self-defeating thoughts such as "You're weak. You're lazy. You're fat. You're stupid. You have no willpower." By this time, I had given my original thought of double-chocolate cake so much energy and attention, that it enveloped me and took on a life of its own. One simple, innocent thought had taken me down into the depths and I truly was feeling bad about myself. All those thoughts of unworthiness and self-hatred were flooding into my mind. I was left feeling hopeless and in despair.

I thought to myself, "Well, just forget it then. Since I already feel horrible about myself, I might as well go ahead and really eat that double-chocolate cake after all." I had expended so much energy, that I was broken and exhausted. I screamed, "I just want the thoughts to stop. I may as well go ahead and eat the cake, just so I can stop thinking about it."

Tired of it all, I dragged myself away from my family, realizing sadly I hadn't really been with them at all. My focus and attention were so consumed by the double-chocolate cake. I walked into the kitchen, opened the refrigerator, pulled out the cake and ate it. After the first bite, I realized that it didn't even taste as good as I had dreamed. In fact, it was actually kind of dry, possibly even stale. It lacked any of the intense, my life. With divine guidance, I shed some loving light on it. I came to the realization that I couldn't continue to binge eat anymore. The shame, the guilt, the destruction was too high a price to pay. I was starting to have serious physical pain and had an awareness that if I didn't stop overeating, that I would die. I was motivated to find a permanent solution to my food challenges. I had faith that the answer was within; that belief never wavered. But I also knew that I needed to get to a deeper level of understanding in order to find the answers once and for all.

As a reminder, the food that I am referring to here is not the kind that is life-giving or fills your heart, soul and body with energy and grace. I will address that food in Part II. I am talking about food that has such a tight and vicious grip on your life that it can interfere with your relationships, your career, your sleep, or your health. It may not be limited to one of those things. It may include all of them.

Taking a closer look, I discovered that I was using excess food to stuff down my heart's desires, aspirations, dreams, wants and needs. I was too afraid to allow them to come to the surface. My fear was that I would be laughed at. The myth for me was that if I spoke up for myself and truly allowed people to see who I really was, then I would be ridiculed and left alone or abandoned. Who was I to go after the things I was truly passionate about? Instead, I sat alone and lonely in my kitchen with food as my companion.

So many times I looked for love in the refrigerator, but

double-chocolate cake or potato chips arise and I find myself being drawn to the kitchen in a trance, I make it a point to stop and remind myself that the answers are not going to be found in there. I literally stop everything that I am doing. If I'm walking, I stop my feet. If I'm talking, I stop my mouth. If I'm holding something, I drop it. I freeze right there.

After I am completely still, I connect with my breath and watch it make its way in and down and then up and out. On the fourth or fifth deep breath, I settle my awareness within, bringing me into the present moment. When I am centered and connected with my innermost truth, then I ask myself the deeper question, "What am I really hungering for?" I use the word "hungering", instead of "hungry", because I know it's not about the food. It's about something much deeper.

It wasn't always easy to find the answer because I had stuffed down the truth for so many years. With practice and constant faith, I gained the courage to explore the deepest places in my heart, peeling away layer after layer. What I was really hungering for led me to honest observations about what was going on in my life at that moment. "Could it be that I think I'm craving the double-chocolate cake because I just had an argument with my husband and I'm looking to soothe myself?" "Could it be that it's not about the food at all, I'm angry at myself for once again repressing my true voice and not allowing my thoughts and feelings to be expressed? I discovered another fear – will I be abandoned?" "Could it be that I'm really craving security right now because I have this morning that you were not going to do it again because you always leave overstuffed, unfulfilled and in disgust with yourself.

When faced with this situation while driving, you can apply the same strategy that we used earlier. First, make a conscious effort to stop all that you are doing. If you are talking on your cell phone, hang up. If you are listening to the radio, turn it off. If you are chewing gum, spit it out. You may even want to pull your car safely into the nearest parking lot and stop, just so you can bring yourself to a complete halt. Once you have made the break from whatever you were doing, connect with your breath following it in and down and up and out. Follow the deep breaths watching them as they rise and fall with the beat of your heart. As you gain your composure from the crazy food thoughts swirling around in your head, ask yourself the deeper question, "What am I really hungering for?"

As you ponder that question, you probe a little deeper with follow-up questions and observations about your day. Inquire lovingly, without judgment or attachment. "Could it be that you're falsely looking to the food for nurturance because you didn't take care of yourself today? You tended to everyone else's needs, yet denied your very own basic existence." "Could it be that you are really looking for security? Did you make a mistake at work today and feel that you are on shaky ground? You can't forgive yourself because you think you should be perfect and never make

The simple question, "What am I really hungering for?" has the power to change your life, along with, your health. Through this process, you will begin to see that it's not about the food and you can stop being at war with it. It's really about your heart's desires, aspirations, dreams, wants and needs. They are desperately trying to unleash themselves into the world. By lovingly addressing what it is you truly desire, you will make peace with your hungry side. You will also be guided on a wonderful and amazing path of self-acceptance, truth and discovery.

> *"We are not born all at once, but by bits."*
> - Mary Antin

CHAPTER FIVE

Crack the Code to Balanced Health

"Just trust yourself, then you will know how to live."
- Johann Wolfgang von Goethe

After focusing my attention and awareness on drastically slowing down the frequency of my binge-eating episodes, I was led to a whole new world of insights and possibilities. The food did not possess me as it once did. However, there were times that my self-defeating thoughts and actions were still getting the best of me.

Thoughts have tremendous power over us. They can either lift us up or tear us down. When we repeat any thought long enough, it takes on a life of its own. Our minds can't distinguish between the *thought* of a major tragedy and the *fact* of a major tragedy. It reacts to both equally. As I became more aware of my thoughts, I was amazed to discover how little time I was truly spending in the present moment. Upon beating myself up. Now I can see why feelings of distress and suffering were familiar to me. I was walking around as a "wounded soul".

Out of that, I began to unravel my thought-process and started to see that when living in the past, there was always a victim and a villain in the stories. When I was the villain, others were the victims and when I was the victim, others were the villains. An example of me playing the victim can be seen in the following familiar thought. "Everyone else gets to eat dessert except me. Why can't I have dessert? Poor me." By telling myself that, I immediately put myself at odds with the people I am with, as well as with the food. Feelings of anger and resentment towards both come to the surface. Then, it also reinforces my feelings of unworthiness and low self-esteem, because subconsciously I'm telling myself I'm not worthy of dessert, but everyone else is. It also brings up feelings of shame and degradation.

Here is an example of another self-defeating thought, but this time I'm playing the villain. "I shouldn't have eaten that." This thought automatically leads me to war with food, making it the victim. I'm also subconsciously telling myself, "I'm bad. I am stupid for having such bad judgment. I'm not allowed to make mistakes. Food is evil." This reinforces feelings of self-hatred, guilt, and shame which puts me in a battle with food. The victim/villain relationship gave me great inspiration to break the cycle because I don't want to be either a victim or a villain.

comes hopelessness, "I really am a loser. I really am fat. I really am stupid. What a failure." I would get myself into such distress over this projection into the future that I might lose weight and then I would subconsciously do something self-destructive to sabotage my efforts. Of course, I would gain the weight back. Whether it was eating foods that were fattening, eating more than I should, or stopping my exercise, I would find a way to bring an end to my weight loss. Needless to say, I even put back on the few pounds I had lost just to be back in my comfort zone.

> *"The thing we fear the most is not that we will*
> *shrivel up and become insignificant little people.*
> *The thing we fear the most is that we could become*
> *as big and grand as we are capable of becoming."*
> - Nelson Mandela

It's truly amazing to me the patterns of destruction I have uncovered in myself. The only reason I am able to reveal them is by grace. As I stay faithful and continue to seek closeness with my innermost core, my blinders slowly start melting away and I'm shown things about myself as I am ready to see them. It's not something I can force or push. This grace is available to everyone who asks to be shown.

It was through observation of my thoughts and actions - without judgment or attachment - that I was guided to create one of the most beneficial tools that I have ever used. This foundation. Quiet your mind and connect with your silent voice on a daily basis. Allow yourself to feel love in and around you every day by taking yourself to a special moment in time where you were one with feelings of love. Live in faith, becoming fully present in the moment. Release feelings and thoughts without judgment or attachment. Now, ever-so-gently come back to your innermost core. Finally, develop an inner acceptance that is always saying "Yes"; just as you know a divine "Yes" is always being said to you. With those vital components, you will unveil the full mystery and sacredness of the four-step process.

> *"God is in the details."*
> - Ludwig Mies van der Rohe

Using my two previous examples as a guide, here is how to *crack the code*:

Example 1: "I shouldn't have eaten that", keeps you stuck in the past.

Example 2: "I'll never be able to lose weight", robs you of your future.

STEP 1: CAPTURE YOUR SELF-DEFEATING THOUGHT.

In this first step, identify and capture one of your self-defeating thoughts. Through the practice of observation, take a look and see if there is a certain event, issue or drama - whether real or imagined – that has been taking up a lot of *and unfulfilling. Things never turn out the way I'd like."*

When you have acknowledged the meaning you have attached to the situation, you will look at the feelings that arise while thinking about it. For instance, does it invoke a feeling of fear, sadness, anger, or loneliness? What are you feeling?

Example 1: I am experiencing a feeling of shame because I ate the food that I shouldn't have eaten. I'm feeling guilty and remorseful. I'm feeling unworthy of any good in my life because I can't do anything right.

Example 2: I am experiencing the feelings of fear, anxiousness and hopelessness because I have convinced myself that if I don't lose weight my future looks bleak. I'll never get the job I want or the family I want and I'll end up alone. I'm having feelings of sadness and apathy because I'll never have the things I truly want and deserve in life.

Now that you have identified the feelings created by the thought, notice how your physical body is reacting. For instance, is your breath getting shorter? Are your shoulders and neck tensing up? Are your palms starting to get sweaty? Are you getting a headache? Make note of all the ways your body is responding to the thought.

Example 1: As I'm thinking about this thought, my body feels heavy

Don't quit before the miracle.
I am worthy and worth it.
I am prepared for this moment.
In faith, I am not afraid.
I find strength in self-surrender.

Example 1: With one breath at a time, I'll give myself the right to be wrong. My greatest lessons are learned through trial and error. I am safe.

Example 2: I trust where I am right now; surrender to where I think I need to be; and know they are one and the same.
Have courage and step forward in faith.

STEP 3: ADMINISTER CARE TO YOURSELF.

One of the most significant steps in this process is also one of the hardest to do. This is the step that has eluded me in the past. It was only when I gained the ability to nurture myself, that I could make the lasting changes leading to weight loss and balanced health. If you truly want a healthy, vibrant, joyous life, you have to start treating yourself better. I can't stress this point enough. I think we don't do nice things for ourselves because we subconsciously think we're not worthy or we're not worth it. You are both worthy and worth it. Start by taking little steps and treat yourself like your best friend or lover. Nobody else can do it for you. You have nothing to lose in this life-affirming experiment and everything to gain.

*"Mothering myself has become
a way of listening to my deepest needs,
and of responding to them while
I respond to my inner child."*
- Melinda Burns

STEP 4: GIVE YOURSELF A REALITY CHECK.

Once you have taken care of yourself and given yourself what you need most in that moment, the final step is to look at the reality of the situation. It's only when we can see our issues with clarity and accuracy that we can release the outcome. This will free us from the mental roller-coaster ride that has kept us in turmoil. This step is very loving and forgiving and should not be a time for shame or disgrace.

*"Since we cannot change reality, let us change
the eyes which see reality."*
- Nikos Kazantzakis

Here are a few ideas that may help you as you create your own reality:

The reality is… I have no control over this situation. If I keep obsessing over it, I am doing great harm to myself physically, emotionally and spiritually.

The reality is… I have no control over other people. They are free to make their own choices.

The reality is… I am doing the best I can with the tools I have at this moment.

The reality is… food isn't going to solve my problems.

Reflections On

CHAPTER FIVE

(The following reflections are offered to you as meditations that will help you nurture and cultivate a deeper connection with your silent voice within. While sitting quietly and breathing slowly and deeply, place your intention on one reflection at a time. Gently clear away thoughts of judgment and attachment, making room for the full mystery and sacredness of the message to permeate your heart and soul.)

~ Living in the past often brings up feelings of anger and guilt.

~ Projecting into the future often evokes feelings of fear, anxiety, and hopelessness.

~ *Cracking the Code* calls upon divine guidance to take over and create balance.

~ The more I practice the four-step method, the easier it becomes.

~ I give myself a beautiful gift each time I walk through the process.

PART TWO

"Keeping your body healthy is an expression of gratitude to the whole cosmos — the trees, the clouds, everything."

- Thich Nhat Hanh

CHAPTER SIX

Listen To Your Body

"The body is a sacred garment. It's your first and last garment;
it is what you enter life in and what you depart life with,
and it should be treated with honor."

- Martha Graham

Creating balanced health is far more than just following another "diet"; it's a celebration of the union between life and spirit. We are all created to be unique and we're given the ability to make wise choices. This ability to choose also applies to food. In order to make intelligent food choices, it's imperative to educate yourself about healthy nutrition.

There are many different roads to obtaining optimal physical health and fitness. I encourage you to explore several of these roads and seek out the path that works best for you. For many years, I have been working on developing and fine-tuning my personal nutrition plan through extensive give you signals to help you fine-tune your personal nutrition plan. Your goal is to have optimal vibrancy and energy. After eating certain foods, take note of how they make you feel. Do these foods leave you feeling tired, foggy-headed, irritated or anxious like you're going to jump out of your skin? Or do they help you feel alive and vibrant and give you an increase of energy? You may certainly get clues about ways to properly feed your body from popular food plans that already exist. These plans can be helpful, but they are only a means to an end. Your silent voice is the ultimate authority that will lead you to the best possible food choices. All you need to do is listen.

One suggestion is to keep a Food Diary to determine which foods are best for your body and which ones make you feel unbalanced. Keep track of how you feel physically, emotionally and spiritually after eating a certain food. Soon, you will see a pattern.

> *"Be aware of the suffering caused*
> *by unmindful consumption."*
> - Thich Nhat Hanh

It's also important to stay in tune with your body when determining a proper serving size. Serving sizes vary because we all have different needs. A 6-foot, 250-pound man is going to have different caloric needs and digestion than a 5-foot, 105-pound woman. Serving sizes also depend on how

Reflections On

CHAPTER SIX

(The following reflections are offered to you as meditations that will help you nurture and cultivate a deeper connection with your silent voice within. While sitting quietly and breathing slowly and deeply, place your intention on one reflection at a time. Gently clear away thoughts of judgment and attachment, making room for the full mystery and sacredness of the message to permeate your heart and soul.)

~ I treat myself with patience and kindness as I discover the right method to nourish my body.

~ I learn to read my body as it reveals the foods that have an unfavorable effect on my health.

~ I keep a Food Diary to see how different foods affect my body.

~ I listen to my body when determining an appropriate serving size.

~ I keep my body super-hydrated by drinking a minimum of 8-to-10 glasses of pure water each day.

~ I will seek help from a health-care practitioner or dietician if I feel it will teach me how to make healthier food choices.

There are lots of books written about the addictive and physical effects certain foods have on your body. I highly recommend that you consider reading them. A few of my favorites include, *Food Addiction: The Body Knows*, and *From The First Bite*, both by Kay Sheppard, M.A. It's important to take command of your body and explore your needs. Balanced health is different for each of us.

As I continue walking my journey of discovery, I notice more often that there are foods that do not support a healthy body. They include sugar, flour, alcohol and caffeine. Whenever I indulge in one of them or a combination of two or more, I feel despondent and lifeless. I know my body is not in balance. When used to excess, these foods make it difficult to have a more intimate and loving relationship with my innermost guide. I can't see the blessings I am receiving because I am in a cloud or fog caused by sugar and flour products. I can't proclaim the magnificence around me because my speech is slurred by alcohol. I can't discern my innermost truth because I am worried about when I can get my next shot of caffeine. The anxiety does not allow me to be peaceful.

When I first realized that I needed to reduce the intake of less desirable foods, I was overcome with fear. "How am I supposed to cut down on foods that I have lived on for months? They are calling my name every second of the day. The foods that numb me out so I can't think straight or feel pain. The foods that give me comfort and keep me company during my hours of need. The foods I spend hours baking, my fears subsided. I chose to set a new course and sail in uncharted territory. This also meant I had to continue drawing hope and inspiration from within.

I began a personal nutrition plan devised with the help of my innermost wisdom. After a few weeks, it felt like a veil was lifted from my eyes and the cobwebs were cleared from my head. The static that had consumed my mind began to get quiet. I began to feel free from the black clouds that had hung over me for so long.

I could now see the world from a different perspective.. I was filled with a lightness and clarity that I had never experienced before. As a result, I felt more peaceful. As I focused on my intentions, my attitude toward food started to shift. Instead of living to eat, I began to eat to live.

The reason diets don't work is because they treat the symptoms, not the underlying cause of the symptoms. Here are some major distinctions between "the diet mind" and "the balanced-health mind":

The diet mind says, "I am restricting my food for a certain amount of time."
The balanced-health mind says, "This is a journey, a lifestyle change that will be achieved one day at a time."

The diet mind says, "I have to have control."
The balanced-health mind says, "I'm giving up control, and allowing my innermost truth to guide me."

Reflections On

CHAPTER SEVEN

(The following reflections are offered to you as meditations that will help you nurture and cultivate a deeper connection with your silent voice within. While sitting quietly and breathing slowly and deeply, place your intention on one reflection at a time. Gently clear away thoughts of judgment and attachment, making room for the full mystery and sacredness of the message to permeate your heart and soul.)

> ~ I eat for balance because it is the key to optimal health and vibrancy.
> ~ Creating balanced health is a celebration of the union between life and spirit.
> ~ I am in command of my body as I continue to explore the best way to nourish and nurture it.
> ~ My innermost truth and wisdom is guiding me to balanced physical health.
> ~ My balanced-health mind knows that this is a journey. I am making a lifestyle change that will be achieved one day at a time.

external object, such as food, drugs, alcohol, or even a person, it controls us. We place it above all else, including the One which gives us life.

On my birthday, I told myself that if I was going to become healthy, the food should taste delicious. I started going through all my old recipe books and altering them to fit my personal nutrition plan. I was able to create appetizing, healthful gourmet meals for my family. The best thing was that I never felt deprived. For the first time, I enjoyed being in the kitchen.

"No one who cooks, cooks alone. Even at her most solitary,
a cook in the kitchen is surrounded by generations of cooks past,
the advice and menus of cooks present,
the wisdom of cookbook writers."
- Laurie Colwin

Whether you have been absent from the kitchen for some time or you are a seasoned chef, you will see a difference when you live in the present moment. Your kitchen will become your sanctuary and safe haven. Before preparing your meals, reflect inward and ask for guidance about which foods will nourish your body. Maximize the potential of your preparation time by lovingly preparing the food. Look at it, touch it, and smell it while you wash, chop, cut and arrange the ingredients.

You might also set the scene with a beautifully decorated table using cloth napkins, candles, flowers, as well as your finest dishes and silverware. As you sit down at the table, take finish everything on your plate, that if you don't eat more now you'll be hungry later, or that you're wasting food. • Those are self-defeating thoughts that no longer support you. Practice living and eating in the present moment, in the here and now. Soon, it will become a habit.

• Food becomes fun when you shift your perception from food as a substitute for feelings and emotions to food as a way to nourish your body. I have learned that food is not my enemy. It's the relationship I had with food that was causing the conflict. I now have respect for such healthful foods as vegetables, fruits, whole grains and proteins. They help nourish and heal my body, which helps me shine at my brightest.

I still treat myself to those foods that I know are less desirable for my body. I have them occasionally, so I don't fall into the trap of perfectionism and deprivation. Now, when I treat myself, I eat the sumptuous food with my full awareness and intention, savoring all the sensual feelings that arise as I eat. I allow the food to bring me great pleasure and enjoyment, as I stay conscious in the moment.

Even with a busy and demanding life, there are ways to get healthy, balanced meals on the table quickly and easily. One of the short cuts I use is to buy a roasted chicken from the grocery store, deli, or as take-out from a restaurant. This makes a great protein selection when you are in a hurry. Another way to save time is to buy vegetables, salads, or plain lettuce that is already pre-washed and chopped in a bag. I like the broccoli-slaw blend or the coleslaw blend available in most supermarkets.

Reflections On

CHAPTER EIGHT

(The following reflections are offered to you as meditations that will help you nurture and cultivate a deeper connection with your silent voice within. While sitting quietly and breathing slowly and deeply, place your intention on one reflection at a time. Gently clear away thoughts of judgment and attachment, making room for the full mystery and sacredness of the message to permeate your heart and soul.)

~ I have fun shopping, preparing and serving food.

~ My kitchen is my sanctuary and safe haven.

~ Before preparing meals, I reflect inward and ask for guidance about which foods are best for my body.

~ I focus only on the food. As I become mindful when I eat, there is no room to add fear, worry or concern.

~ I rely on my innermost truth to guide me so I know there is no room for guilt or shame.

from the experience, make adjustments and move forward with compassion.

When I first started listening to my innermost wisdom, I was afraid to leave the safety and security of my kitchen. My husband loves going out to dinner and I knew that he was not going to be happy sitting at home forever – even if I was becoming a great cook. It was time to face my fear and get out of my comfort zone, and I had to do this quickly. I had to come up with a way to accommodate both of our needs. Looking back, I'm glad I was pushed out the door because it helped me to develop some useful coping techniques. These were a blessing because I discovered that they made our time together even more pleasant.

At first, I was a little scared and unsure of myself. I felt like a new baby taking her first steps. Soon, I developed confidence and learned to be very clear about my desires and expectations for the evening.

One way to achieve that is by setting your intention for the experience. You can do this through prayer or quiet contemplation *before* you leave your home. Setting an intention for the evening helps you to make a connection with your innermost truth. For example, you might set an intention to go out and have a great time without being too concerned about what you eat or drink. If so, do it with your whole self and be present in the moment. If your intention is to enjoy the company and eat healthy foods that serve your body, then stay mindful and present when you order your meal. Focus the threat of overeating or indulging in something that is not healthy.

During my process of discovery, I also learned three very important words, "No, thank you." Use these powerful words when you are tempted with an extra helping of food, the cookies for an afternoon snack, or the dessert after dinner. It became easier the more I heard myself saying this simple, polite phrase.

Before I discovered the power of saying, "No, thank you," I never passed up anything that was offered to me. I thought I would hurt another person's feelings if I didn't try whatever they were offering me. I have discovered that this type of thinking is actually a demonstration of ego and grandiosity. I would hope that the other person did not give me that much power or influence over their life. I had such illusions of grandeur to think that if I said, "No" to whatever they were offering me, it would upset the delicate balance of their life.

I had to ask myself, "Did I give this much power to other people when I offered them something to eat?" How did I feel when someone told me, "No, thank you?" I like to feel that I am important to other people; but when I turned it around, it helped to put it in perspective.

I encourage you to follow your heart when making a choice to accept a treat or say, "No, thank you." You may decide to say, "Yes" and eat what is offered to you. Maybe you truly desire it and have made the conscious decision to accept and enjoy it. Don't eat because you have feelings of guilt or a sense little intimidated by the server when I would make any special requests. It finally dawned on me that if I didn't speak up for myself, nobody else would. I started getting very clear about the intentions I had set and began to take a pro-active role. I learned to ask questions about the ingredients used in certain foods. If they weren't pleasing to my body, I passed them up. This can be done with grace and help from your innermost guide. With faith, you can learn to make healthier choices.

Restaurants become willing to accommodate your needs if they are customer-service oriented. There is a lot of competition for your business. When you order your meal, feel confident that they will serve you exactly what you want. If you have a positive attitude and know that you can get what you desire, then you will see it happen. You will become savvy at reading the menu and begin to quickly sort through the different choices. If you find it less stressful, you can call the restaurant ahead of time to work out your needs.

Before you open the menu, center yourself by following your breath inward and down. As you begin to relax, silently ask for guidance and wisdom to choose an appropriate food item. By making that connection first, you will gain confidence and clarity in order to make healthy choices.

Another challenge we face when dining out is the large portion size that most restaurants like to serve. Try to use the same serving size that you learned to use at home. One be okay if I brought a few items that I could eat. "Absolutely, no problem," was what she told me. I had needlessly worried about it prior to the dinner, because my assumption was that everyone would think I was weird. I based this conclusion on the fact that I would be eating something different from everyone else. I wanted to fit in and not draw attention to myself. All that worrying was a waste of time because when we sat down for dinner, everyone put food on their plate and no one even noticed that I was eating something completely different from the planned menu. As we drove home that night, I was laughing to myself because I finally realized that I was the only one who was pre-occupied or obsessed with what I was eating.

TRAVELING:

I have always loved to travel and I wanted to continue traveling whenever I had an opportunity. I did not want my new eating plan to stop me from going away if I had an opportunity to do so. With some thought, planning, and preparation, you can make just about any trip free of food stress.

I try to eliminate unnecessary stress on the actual travel day by preparing a meal at home and bringing it with me. If you have healthy food with you, you will remove some of the anxiety of an already-busy day. When you are hungry, you don't have to try and find something healthy in an airport or bus station. I'm sure you will also prepare a tastier meal than you could buy in a fast-food restaurant. It is usually

Reflections On

CHAPTER NINE

(The following reflections are offered to you as meditations that will help you nurture and cultivate a deeper connection with your silent voice within. While sitting quietly and breathing slowly and deeply, place your intention on one reflection at a time. Gently clear away thoughts of judgment and attachment, making room for the full mystery and sacredness of the message to permeate your heart and soul.)

~ When I live fully, life becomes an adventure.
   I feel free to explore and grow.

~ I set my intention for an experience before
   I leave home.

~ In order to stay centered while away from
   home, I keep an inspirational saying or prayer
   in my pocket or purse.

~ Just for today, I will politely say, "No, thank
   you" to food that is not healthy for my body.

~ I will release any illusions of grandeur along with
   the magic I have given to that one bite.

~ I am expanding my horizons and becoming a
   light to all I meet.

means you might need to make a different choice next time.

Change can happen rapidly – as in the split second that will change someone's life forever – or it may come in incremental steps so that your body, mind and spirit have a chance to adapt more easily. It could occur after a shift in your thinking or a shift in your actions. It may even start internally and has not yet shown up at the external level. However and whenever change shows up in your life, know that it all is perfect for your journey. At times, it might even feel like you are taking a step backward. Trust in your innermost wisdom to lead you to your highest and best good. Always be open to all possibilities and embrace even the smallest smattering of change.

If you didn't get the results you were looking for previously, learn from those choices. The key is to never, ever give up on yourself. When you make a serious commitment to transform, it will happen; not necessarily in your time table, but it will happen. Those who actively attempt to make changes in their lives are ultimately successful, though it may take some course corrections along the way.

> *"It is the soul's duty to be loyal to its own desires.*
> *It must abandon itself to its master passion."*
> - Rebecca West

When you invite change into your life, allow it to begin with an awareness of the divine presence within. Every welcomes change into your life. Take an opportunity to look at and examine what you truly desire. Be specific about your wishes and dreams. Clearly see the outcome. Act as if the change has already been accomplished. Feel the change that is happening in your body. Hear the change as you speak to yourself in a new and loving way.

The second motivator is to have a clear purpose established for the change. List specific reasons why you must see this through to completion. Then, list all the good things that will come from the change. Also, assess your personal need for this change by asking yourself why this change is so important to you. What is the meaning that you have attached to the change?

The third way to motivate yourself is to know that you are not alone on this journey of transformation. You always have your loving and trusted companion walking with you toward your goal. Reflect inward and feel the presence of divinity deep within.

If you know other people who are walking a spiritual journey to balanced health, support them as they learn new behaviors. Conversely, be open to help and support from friends and family. Ask for what you need. There is strength in consciousness when two or more are gathered... this is where miracles happen.

You can make changes in your life by being willing to listen to guidance from within and to follow wherever you are led. When you do, get ready to live life to the fullest. Your

Reflections On

CHAPTER TEN

(The following reflections are offered to you as meditations that will help you nurture and cultivate a deeper connection with your silent voice within. While sitting quietly and breathing slowly and deeply, place your intention on one reflection at a time. Gently clear away thoughts of judgment and attachment, making room for the full mystery and sacredness of the message to permeate your heart and soul.)

~ I invite change into my life and I move forward in faith.

~ I am free to choose.

~ When I am centered in the Divine and open to guidance, I can invite any form of positive change into my life.

~ I choose to become the change I wish to see in the world.

PART THREE

"God, grant me the serenity
to accept the things I cannot change;
Courage to change the things I can;
And, wisdom to know the difference."

-The Serenity Prayer, Dr. Reinhold Niebuhr

INTRODUCTION TO

ఠ THE PRINCIPLES ఠ

"Sometimes in your life you will go on a journey.
It will be the longest journey you have ever taken.
It is the journey to find yourself."
- Katherine Sharp

Have you ever noticed that you can learn your greatest lessons when you are most desperate and vulnerable?

When I was in the midst of what seemed like a difficult and dark time in my life, I planted seeds that would help me grow and blossom as I became healthy. Each seed, that I planted during my seeming 'failures', has become one of *The 12 Spiritual Principles of Balanced Health.* I wanted to discover the "real" me, even if it frightened me to look at what I was at that point in my life. Often, I struggled because I didn't like what I was seeing. I wanted to fight and curse and accuse someone else of making me miserable. I certainly did not want to take responsibility for my mistakes and lack of judgment.

I screamed passionately, "I am afraid to look within." I had this daunting feeling that something was going to crack, and it would probably be me. "Am I going mad?" I whispered softly as I peered around in the darkness, not really

At the end of each Principle, there is a section called "Gifts of Awareness". This section will include special questions to help you unveil the presence of divinity in your life. Each question in the "Gifts of Awareness" section relates to a Principle. It is helpful to use a journal when you answer these questions.

Before beginning the "Gifts of Awareness" section, get into a space that allows you to open up to your full awareness. Take time to unite with your silent voice within. When you connect, you gain insights and understanding that you were unaware of in the past. I like to think of these as 'aha' moments. They are revelations that you probably would not have discovered without inner wisdom to guide you.

If you would like additional direction in choosing a method to use when connecting with your center, refer back to Chapter Two.

complete control. It was only when I let go and set an intention to succeed in my life-altering changes, that I was finally able to get off the dieting merry-go-round.

Before undergoing any changes, I encourage you to be still and listen. Search your motives by asking yourself this question, "Am I seeking changes in my life based on my ego-based self or am I seeking changes to honor and glorify divinity within me?" If you are patient and persistent, the truth will be revealed to you. Don't be discouraged if you think it's a slow process, because everything happens in perfect timing.

> *"Everyone who wills can hear the inner voice.*
> *It is within everyone."*
> - Mahatma Gandhi

Once you determine that you are going to shift your life to one of balanced health, then also choose the willingness to carry it out. Make a clear, conscious decision to act and move forward in faith. Never regret and never look back.

If you allow yourself to be guided from within, you will unlock the doors to your destiny. This may reveal a life that is full of exciting, unseen possibilities. By trusting your inner guidance and taking the actions necessary to move forward, you can create the space for change. If you thought you were lacking in strength, faith, courage, hope or determination, you will be filled to overflowing with these characteristics. All it takes is a small amount of willingness, even as small as the size of one grain of

Reflections On

PRINCIPLE ONE

(The following reflections are offered to you as meditations that will help you nurture and cultivate a deeper connection with your silent voice within. While sitting quietly and breathing slowly and deeply, place your intention on one reflection at a time. Gently clear away thoughts of judgment and attachment, making room for the full mystery and sacredness of the message to permeate your heart and soul.)

- ~ I choose willingness and follow the calling of my innermost truth.
- ~ I move forward in trust and faith.
- ~ I create the space for change every day.
- ~ I am filled and over-flowing. There is always abundance.
- ~ I receive the gifts of faith, hope, strength, courage, forgiveness and acceptance when I am willing to listen to divine guidance.
- ~ There is no turning back. The time is now!

of Willingness and remind yourself that you choose to be willing to listen. I encourage you to light a candle as a symbol that you are expressing your commitment.

F. Are you willing to open your heart to your innermost truth, wherever you are led? Why do you feel willing now?

G. Write down any concerns, fears, and worries that you have at this time. Then, write down your hopes and dreams.

H. Are you ready to step forward? Are you willing to create a new life of balanced health?

You feel as if there is something deeper that is making you eat more than you need to for balanced nutrition or eat foods that are not healthy for you. However, you aren't sure what it is that causes this behavior.

In Principle Two, you are going to look at these challenges for what they really are. You might learn things about yourself that have been concealed your entire life. Sometimes, they are buried so deeply that you have hidden them from yourself, as well as from others. Allow yourself plenty of time to remember events that have been covered up for a long time. Don't forget to be gentle with yourself and proceed with a loving, open heart.

"There is a gold mine within you from which
you can extract everything you need to live life
gloriously, joyously, and abundantly."
- Joseph Murphy

One way to get an accurate account about your relationship with food, your body and your weight is to write a brief history, outlining key events that relate to these issues. This is a loving exercise, not something you are doing to make yourself feel guilty.

Be honest with yourself and write about your feelings regarding your body, the diets you've tried, and how much weight you've lost or gained up until now. I encourage you to be thoughtful and thorough as you write about your past.

that time. It was very obvious to see food as a challenge in my life. This had not always been so clear to me. It hit me squarely between the eyes once I examined my history. For the first time, I was able to see my pattern of self-destruction. I turned to food instead of facing any issues I should have been dealing with at that time. Once I put the words on paper, I was able to see it and believe it.

Don't worry about using proper grammar or punctuation when you are writing your history. Just put your thoughts on paper. This is not for anyone else to read if you don't want to share it; it is mainly for your benefit. There is no 'right' or 'wrong' way to journal. The important thing is to begin where you are in your life right now.

Gifts of Awareness

PRINCIPLE TWO

(Gifts of Awareness are special questions that will help you unveil the presence of divinity in your life. Answer these questions in a personal journal and at your own pace. They are pearls of wisdom and discovery that are revealed during the process of transformation. They are available to you as a guide along your journey. During this time, practice being loving and gentle with yourself. By being tolerant and accepting toward yourself and others, you create the space for change.)

A. Write down the major incidents or events in your life that you relate to food, your body, and your weight.

B. What was your relationship with food when you were a child? Did you feel differently about your body as a child than you do as an adult? How so?

C. Does food, by itself, become a significant event in your family? What does food mean to you? What feelings are associated with food?

D. Make a list of all the different diets you have been on. How much weight have you lost and gained in the past?

༜ PRINCIPLE THREE ༜

Reflect Inward

*"Ask and it will be given to you; seek and you will find;
knock and the door will be opened to you.
For everyone who asks receives; he who seeks finds;
and to him who knocks, the door will be opened."*
- Luke 11:9, 10.

In May 1997, I desperately shouted, "God, help me! Please help me!" My journey to consciousness began with those small, yet very powerful words. As I reflect on that experience, I realized that help was there all along. It was patiently waiting for me in the stillness, knowing that one day I would ask for it. I heard the sweet, loving words stir from within saying, "I know you are scared, child. Just take my hand."

When I finally surrendered, I connected with the infinite power of love. When you stop trying to control what is happening in my soul could only be satiated by one thing – and that was the grace of God – without which my healing would never have taken place.

If talking to your silent voice is something that makes you feel awkward or does not seem natural, just imagine yourself having a warm and engaging conversation with a dear friend. Speak in the words you would normally use when talking to someone else. The words don't have to be said in a perfect voice or spoken in "prayer language"; just allow them to come from your heart. If all you can say is, "God, help me", that is a powerful place to start.

"Whatever you can do or dream you can, begin it;
Boldness has genius, power and magic in it."
- Johann Wolfgang von Goethe

The root idea of Principle Three is *faith*. You demonstrate your faith when you ask to be guided by a divine presence. You recognize that you are being led down a different path and will be granted a new beginning. No matter how far you think you are from where you wish to be, the journey begins when you have faith in something greater than yourself to lead you back to health. Never feel that your life is helpless or hopeless; simply ask that your faith be restored.

When I reflected inward to the depths of my soul, and looked to my innermost source of love and wisdom, I knew that my body would return to wholeness. Prior to that day, I never thought to look within as I dealt with my food challenges.

Gifts of Awareness

PRINCIPLE THREE

(Gifts of Awareness are special questions that will help you unveil the presence of divinity in your life. Answer these questions in a personal journal and at your own pace. They are pearls of wisdom and discovery that are revealed during the process of transformation. They are available to you as a guide along your journey. During this time, practice being loving and gentle with yourself. By being tolerant and accepting toward yourself and others, you create the space for change.)

A. In your journal, write about *your* best efforts to control your food and weight. What results have you experienced?

B. Where are you today - on a scale of 1 to 10 (10 being best) - with your health and vibrancy? Your weight? Your body image?

C. Are you now willing to reflect inward to find help in achieving balanced health?

D. Take time to ask for a new beginning. Ask that your heart and mind be open to change. Ask also to be willing and able to see, feel and hear things differently from now on. Ask to be given guidance for your journey. If you feel helpless or hopeless, ask that your faith be restored.

You can develop your own *Declaration of Truth* by spending quiet time observing your passions, dreams and desires. Your *Declaration* is a discovery of the answers or pictures you receive in the meditation. It becomes a road map to your future. It is a bigger version of your day-to-day life where you consider your values and core beliefs.

To begin, close your eyes and take a few slow, deep breaths. As you follow your breath, allow your awareness to settle within, uniting with your innermost truth. When you feel relaxed, ask that you be shown the person you will become. Spend some time thinking about yourself in the highest and best vision that you can create. With trust, along with your renewed faith, walk forward into this new life that you are designing. Ask that you be shown your destiny, purpose, passion, or contribution to the universe. This is your chance to discover your mission and learn about the person you've always wanted to become. You can achieve anything your heart desires.

As you are watching yourself through a new set of eyes, take detailed mental notes of the person you are becoming. Allow your mind to soar; the sky is the limit to what you can visualize. Don't discount or dismiss anything.

Make notes after you complete the meditation. Write about how you are feeling living the life of your dreams. How do you look? How do you walk and talk? Do you stand a bit straighter or taller? How do people treat you? How do you treat others? Are you humble? Are you grateful? Are you possible. Do not be concerned if others don't understand or approve of what you have stated in your *Declaration*. This is a process between you and your infinite power, not between you and anyone else.

I will share my *Declaration* with you in order for you to have an example. Once my *Declaration* was complete, I enlarged several copies to the size of a poster and had it laminated. I hung them in strategic places in order to continually connect with the true person that I am.

BRONWYN'S DECLARATION OF TRUTH

In divinity, I am humility.
By grace, I am guided and committed
to living in harmony with my innermost truth.
With the strength and courage of my infinite power,
I passionately spread the message of balanced health.
With my creator receiving all the glory,
I am recognized for changing lives.
Through the wisdom of my innermost being,
I am efficient, professional and creative.
With the devotion of my innermost spirit,
I am committed and faithful to family.
With infinite love, I am love and compassion for all.
In God, I am complete.

When I read my *Declaration of Truth*, it feeds my soul. Each word is extremely powerful and produces a series of *am love and compassion for all."* Through the love and compassion I receive from my innermost being, I am filled-up with a never-ending well of love. I do not need to be afraid to share all that is in my heart and soul. Finally, *"In God, I am complete"*. I acknowledge the totality and wholeness of God which is in me and around me. We are inseparable. I am a perfect and complete child of my creator.

Create your *Declaration* as a way to express your innermost faith. Your statement can take on any form that works for you. Mine is only one example. If you would like additional ideas on writing your *Declaration of Truth*, visit www.BronwynMarmo.com. Just click on *Declare Your Truth* to see more examples. You will also have the opportunity to share your *Declaration* with others.

After you have completed your writing, make several copies so that one is available to you anytime you want to read it. Keep a copy with you and read it throughout the day. This will help you connect with the incredible person you are right now.

Gifts of Awareness

PRINCIPLE FOUR

(Gifts of Awareness are special questions that will help you unveil the presence of divinity in your life. Answer these questions in a personal journal and at your own pace. They are pearls of wisdom and discovery that are revealed during the process of transformation. They are available to you as a guide along your journey. During this time, practice being loving and gentle with yourself. By being tolerant and accepting toward yourself and others, you create the space for change.)

A. Write down the things you have been shown about
    the person you are. Capture the feelings and emotions
    of the life you've always dreamed about. Write in the
    present tense, "I am… ". You are that person right
    now, whether you can see it or feel it at this time.

B. Using the information you collected, start creating
    your *Declaration of Truth*. Your statement can take on
    any form that works for you. Create it, enjoy it, and
    allow it to speak to your soul.

C. You may also choose to create a "Collage of Truth".
    This is a fun way of displaying your innermost truth.
    I created mine from my favorite magazines. Simply
    cut out certain pictures and quotations that inspire

PRINCIPLE FIVE

Practice Being Imperfect

"Perfectionism is the voice of the oppressor,
the enemy of the people.
It will keep you cramped and insane your whole life."
- Anne Lamott

Creating a life of balanced health means actively pursuing progress - not perfection. Know that you are exactly where you need to be right now. Faith and trust allow you to be shaped and molded, as if you are a piece of clay. The pursuit of perfection can rob you of feeling complete love and truth. If you set your sights on perfection, you miss out on all the divine beauty that is present along your path. You become rigid, not allowing the light to shine through the cracks. You will never feel happy, joyous and free because perfection is elusive and thus, can never be achieved.

Several years after I had released my weight, I noticed

I squeezed the girdle up over my thighs, continuing to pull and tug, until it went over my stomach and up and over my breasts. I had to hold my breath because the girdle was so tight. It also felt like it was pinching my ribs together.

Once I had the girdle in place, I put on my favorite sweater and ran to the mirror. I looked at myself in the front and exclaimed, "Wow! This looks great." Then, I turned around in horror and saw the view from the back. I almost died of shock because the roll of fat had strategically squeezed its way up my back and was now across my shoulders, sitting just above the girdle. It looked like I was carrying a big long salami with the thick roll of skin, and it was perched right on top of my back. I looked like the Hunch Back of Notre Dame. I was so disappointed because my brilliant plan had failed. I was crushed as I took off the girdle. I planned to return them to the store and put this whole fiasco behind me.

I walked out to the kitchen where I found my husband preparing his lunch. Before I had a chance to say anything, he said in a sarcastic tone of voice, "So, I understand you just spent $185 on underwear." I was shocked, wondering, "How did he know?" I hadn't told anyone what I had done. He proceeded to tell me that the credit card company's Fraud Protection Department called because they thought it was suspicious that someone would spend $185 on underwear and they wanted to verify the purchase. I couldn't believe it. Of all the purchases I have ever made, they chose this one to call for verification. I was mortified.

perfection. Of course, I could never achieve it; so I was always feeling bad about myself. I tried to demand perfection from myself and those around me. I had created an illusion that everything in my life was "perfect". I was "perfect". I had a "perfect" marriage, body, clothing size, children, house and job.

I blamed everyone around me when things weren't going my way. I was holding myself up to a standard that could never be achieved. Deep down, I really felt inferior. I didn't allow myself to make mistakes and I constantly beat myself up for any mistakes I had made. Even knowing how much I was loved, it wasn't enough for me to love myself.

I set out on a journey of discovering authentic self-love. I wanted to love myself as much as I knew I was loved. I wanted to see my beauty and talents through the eyes of my soul. When I followed my own agenda, I felt miserable and depressed. I realized that the answers to finding authentic self-love, forgiveness and acceptance were not going to come from an outside source. I could get several tummy tucks or have liposuction or buy lots of girdles and still not feel any better about myself. The only place left to look was inward and enlist the help of my innermost consciousness.

When I searched inside, I was surprised to discover that I was harboring cruel and harsh feelings. I ruthlessly viewed my "old self" as a "fat, disgusting pig". My intuition told me that I needed to repair the relationship that I had with my "old self", and bridge the gap between her and the woman I

As I wrote the letter, I imagined two women - one was me today and one was me from yesterday. They were holding hands as the Bronwyn of Today walked the Bronwyn of Yesterday through her life to show her that everything she experienced was divinely planned for her highest and best self to emerge. She informed her that there is total forgiveness for her unskilled behavior in the past. Then, Today's Woman nurtured and comforted Yesterday's Woman by cradling her in her arms. It was as if she was a newborn being rocked in a rocking chair. I could feel the deep, unconditional love being shared as Today's Woman stroked the forehead of Yesterday's Woman and assured her that everything would be all right.

My thoughts began to shift as the two women were standing and locked in a tight embrace. Both were drawing strength and courage from each other. It was as if they knew that one could not survive without the other one. They made each other feel complete through their love and support.

It was an emotional experience for me to write the letter. It was healing since it helped me see that it was necessary for me to be the Woman of Yesterday in order to be the Woman I am Today. Once I internalized that concept, and embraced the old me; I was able to find compassion and forgiveness for what I thought were my mistakes.

After that experience, I discovered a deeper self-love because this time it was generated by a love that surpassed my own. I was able to love myself, the way I was loved message that I know better than my infinite power.

Instead, I celebrate and honor the function of each of my body's parts. I recognize that my stomach area isn't flat because it carried my precious children. It helped enable new life to come into the world. These incredible little beings have brought me joy and happiness. I see my broad shoulders and strong arms as necessary to give them big "bear hugs". They also can protect and shield my children from harm.

What I learned from that experience was that I was diminishing my capacity to love because I was coming from a position of loathing and negativity. I was also not able to fully love my children, husband, or friends. How could I completely love them if I didn't even love myself? What was also disheartening to me was that my self-loathing was minimizing my ability to love my innermost guide and be open to the abundant graces that were being laid before me.

With the help of divine love that is always available to you, you can rejoice in your freedom and let go of self-abuse. You can love and forgive yourself; then, become proud of the steps you are making toward balanced health. A positive attitude and forward movement will be rewarded with abundant grace and guidance to lead you into a new life.

It may be a challenge for you to love yourself if you include your imperfections. You may think that if you love yourself too much the way you are right now, then you might become complacent or comfortable. This could stop you from wanting to pursue a life of balanced health. In reality, it's

Reflections On

PRINCIPLE FIVE

(The following reflections are offered to you as meditations that will help you nurture and cultivate a deeper connection with your silent voice within. While sitting quietly and breathing slowly and deeply, place your intention on one reflection at a time. Gently clear away thoughts of judgment and attachment, making room for the full mystery and sacredness of the message to permeate your heart and soul.)

~ I accept imperfection as a part of life.

~ The pursuit of perfection robs me of feeling complete love and truth.

~ I am comfortable in my body.

~ I love myself the same way that my creator loves me.

~ I am healing the relationship that I have with my "old self".

~ I love my body just the way it is and the way it is not.

F. Are you at peace with the "You of Yesterday"? If not, how can you heal the relationship?

G. Write a letter to your "old self". It can take any form you wish and still be the right way for you. You may want to write it on beautiful stationery.

H. How do you take care of yourself and show that you love yourself?

more grace will be given to you.

You are special and are rewarded simply for being alive. Believing and trusting that you are blessed beyond belief takes time to accept, but you can get started right now. All you have to do is focus on your blessings. It's important to remind yourself every day of the gifts that are yours as soon as you claim them. Ignore the things you don't have in your life and focus on what you do have. More will be added as you practice this every day.

"Gratitude unlocks the fullness of life.
It turns what we have into enough, and more.
It turns denial into acceptance, chaos to order,
confusion to clarity."
- Melody Beattie

One way to bring positive aspects into focus is by creating your own blessings journal. It's easy - list all the things you are grateful for in your life as it is right now. At first, you may find it hard to come up with even a few things. You may not be feeling very appreciative right now. You also might be feeling depressed regarding your food choices and health. You may know that strength and willpower alone are not enough to win this battle; and that you must look inside yourself for help. You might not be willing to do the work required to make lasting changes in your life.

When I began my work, I was overwhelmed, angry and

By embracing grace, you are forced to rely on something greater than yourself. Your heart, mind and soul will expand beyond what you thought possible, and the whole world opens up to receive you. One way to begin embracing grace is to focus on all the things you are grateful for right now in your life. Start with one thing on your list, and watch it grow. The more blessings you focus on, the more strength and power you will draw from them. When you have a bad day and you slip back into negativity, stop – review your list of blessings and say, "My life isn't so bad. In fact, I really enjoy it most of the time. Look at all the things I have to be grateful for. This too shall pass."

Writing your list of blessings provides you with a bottomless supply of love, joy and happiness. Make a choice and commitment every day to receive the gifts so readily available to you. You will need strength for your journey. If you make room in your heart for love and joy, you will remain full of hope and courage as your body is changing. With strength, and help from within, you can achieve your heart's desires.

Add to your blessings journal every day. You can use it as a gauge to see your emotional and spiritual progress. If your list is growing abundantly, then you know you are on the right track and filled with grace. If you are struggling to find blessings in your life, sit quietly and ask to be shown what they are at this time.

Gifts of Awareness

PRINCIPLE SIX

(Gifts of Awareness are special questions that will help you unveil the presence of divinity in your life. Answer these questions in a personal journal and at your own pace. They are pearls of wisdom and discovery that are revealed during the process of transformation. They are available to you as a guide along your journey. During this time, practice being loving and gentle with yourself. By being tolerant and accepting toward yourself and others, you create the space for change.)

A. In a separate journal, designated to capture your blessings, make a list of all the things you are grateful for right now. Continue listing your blessings every day.

B. Go back to your Gifts of Awareness journal and write in detail about one person or thing you are most grateful for right now.

C. Who do you love? Make a list of their qualities. Who loves you?

D. Do you have negative attitudes or thinking that stand in your way or hinder your faith? If so, what are they?

E. Do you feel worthy of the incredible grace you are being given? Why or why not?

DIALOGUE WITH DIVINITY:

One way to engage in dialogue with the divine presence is to close your eyes and go within. Imagine you are in the midst of the most beautiful sight you've ever seen. Notice every aspect of your surroundings: the shapes, the figures, the colors, the sounds. Then, outstretch your hand as you feel yourself being gently pulled forward. You will be softly and lovingly led from one situation to the next throughout your day.

As you stay close, you proceed to ask questions, such as, "What is Your will for me?" When you come across a challenging situation with someone, you can ask, "How can I resolve this problem so that the outcome is the best for everyone concerned?" If you're having difficulty making a decision, ask, "Which direction do You want me to take?"

"Seek not outside yourself, heaven is within."
- Mary Lou Cook

I use the same process when I'm preparing my meals. I ask a lot of questions. While in the kitchen, I stay especially mindful and thoughtful, and ask questions such as, "What healthy, balanced foods would You like to see me eat today?" "What can I prepare for my family that would most please You?" "Do I have the proper serving size of protein, vegetables and quality carbohydrate-rich foods to nourish my body?" The answer is always there. I just need to be open to hearing it.

while walking or you can sit comfortably in a chair at home. Any time or place works as long as you can hear the silence.

Take time every day for reflection. As you continue to quiet your mind, you expand the space for stillness. This will allow you to "hear" your innermost wisdom. Answers will be revealed to you; sometimes quickly, sometimes slowly. Sometimes it's the answer you want; sometimes it's not. You have to trust and affirm that you are walking with your trusted companion. No one else can give you a true and accurate answer about what's best for you.

Answers come to you in many different ways and it will take time to trust your innermost consciousness. Guidance may come in the way of a new concept, an inspiration, or a change of heart or attitude. It may come through other people who have been placed in your path – seemingly by chance. One of the best ways to determine if you are actually hearing the "voice of love" is to observe how the information you receive affects you. If you once were angry and resentful, you are now peaceful; if you once were revengeful and felt hatred towards someone, you now are feeling love; if you once swore that you could never reduce the intake of unhealthy foods, you now are willing to try. These feelings are all signs that you have heard your innermost truth.

My meditation time is a priority because it is so inspiring and enriching. I schedule it as part of my day and block out the time in my organizer. I have found that quiet time does not happen by accident. It is a space we create because we

Then, ponder the meaning and ask, "How does it apply to my life today?" This is a powerful approach because you are being guided to discover what you need to see on that particular day.

Seek out Sacred Scripture when you are searching for answers to a problem. If it works for you, read encouraging and uplifting text when you are struggling with food issues. If you are craving something that you know is not good for you, or if you want to eat larger portions than usual; turn to books that are divinely inspired. They can bring you comfort and strength to stay on your path. By taking a few minutes to reconnect with your innermost being, you will be rewarded with a soothing and tranquil feeling. The craving, which originally seemed so intense, will wash over you like surf along the beach. Try it the next time you are experiencing food challenges.

Another way of raising your consciousness and awareness is to get involved in a book study group with others who are walking a spiritual path. Listening to another person's interpretation of the book and how they incorporated the lessons they learned into their lives is helpful to me. Every time you read Sacred Scripture and inspirational books you will be opening your heart further and learning about yourself on an intimate level.

JOURNAL YOUR JOURNEY:

As you proceed on your journey to balanced health, I

Reflections On

PRINCIPLE SEVEN

(The following reflections are offered to you as meditations that will help you nurture and cultivate a deeper connection with your silent voice within. While sitting quietly and breathing slowly and deeply, place your intention on one reflection at a time. Gently clear away thoughts of judgment and attachment, making room for the full mystery and sacredness of the message to permeate your heart and soul.)

~ I seek divine direction on a daily basis.

~ I nurture my soul through prayer, meditation, journaling and reading.

~ I dialogue with divinity and acknowledge that I need guidance.

~ I harmonize with my heart. The answer is always available and I'm open to hearing it.

~ I learn about my innermost guide by reading and studying Sacred Scripture and inspiring books.

~ I journal about my journey because writing helps me reveal my heart's innermost desires, as well as my frustrations.

౬౯ PRINCIPLE EIGHT ౫౩

Bless Your Balanced Health

"Spiritual relationship is far more precious than physical.
Physical relationship divorced from spiritual is body without soul."
- Mahatma Gandhi

When you receive guidance that will lead you to balanced health, you are receiving the gifts of courage, strength and willingness. The guidance will come and show you possibilities that you have never seen before.

BE GRATEFUL FOR YOUR FOOD:

One way to create balanced health is to invite input from your innermost wisdom. Ask this wisdom what you should eat that will give you the optimal energy so you can carry out your life's passion. Take a few minutes to prayerfully write out a menu of the food you will be eating for the day. As you are planning your meals, open up to the guidance that is present within you and beautiful gift to give yourself as you retire for the night.

I like to prayerfully write my nutrition plan for the next day before I go to bed. That helps me in two ways: First, it forces me to make sure I have all the ingredients I need for the next day's meals, and second, it keeps me focused on the abundant and beautiful meal that I will be eating in the morning. When I wake up, I'm not tempted to think about or eat anything else.

DINE WITH YOUR HONORED GUEST:

Another way to include awareness in a balanced and healthy lifestyle is to invite your honored guest to join you at every meal. Imagine sitting at the table when your meal is set before you. Before you begin to eat, breathe very slowly and get into a relaxed state. Watch your breath as it settles down just below your navel.

Eat slowly as you think of questions you'd like to ask your inner wisdom. Then, sit quietly and wait for the answers. Stay focused while you eat, so you don't get caught up in the food. Your every need is already satisfied when you give your internal barometer a chance.

"The table is a meeting place, a gathering ground,
the source of sustenance and nourishment, festivity,
safety and satisfaction."

- Laurie Colwin

I know mealtime can get overwhelming and stressful. That's also a reason to dine with an honored guest. You can still engage in conversation with your family, yet keep coming back to your center. You may not always do it perfectly and that's all right. The point is to know where to turn in any challenging situation.

MOVE WITH THE FLOW:

Exercise is an important part of any health program, but you don't have to spend hours a day in the gym. That is not balance. Exercise is merely moving your body in the way it was intended to be moved. Movement is a natural and basic part of life. It can be as simple as walking, running, bicycling, hiking, golfing, playing tennis, swimming laps or playing in the pool. It can be anything that you enjoy and keeps your movement fluid.

Exercise builds lean muscle mass which helps burn fat. It is something that almost everyone can do. Just start out slowly and gradually increase your intensity. You will build up your strength and stamina and make fitness a priority. It's a good idea to consult a doctor before beginning an exercise program.

When you first start, you may not like to exercise. It might be hard work trying to move. You might have to exert a lot of energy and could get exhausted by simple things such as going up and down the stairs. It may seem easier to lie on the couch and watch TV.

your interests or desires, just get out there and move. You can make it a family affair. Exercising is a perfect way to spend time with family and friends.

RELEASE YOUR WEIGHT:

Release your weight instead of "lose" your weight. I know I haven't "lost" 50 pounds, because that implies that I don't know where the excess weight went. I know exactly where that weight went. Just as I release my food and my body, I also release my weight. I have such peace of mind and comfort because I know I'm being cared for in the best possible way. Also, when I speak of "losing" weight, the message to my subconscious mind is: "Alert! Bronwyn has lost something. We *must* replace it."

It's important to remember that as you release your weight, you are also releasing all pre-conceived ideas of a goal weight. You are now free of the scale because it just doesn't matter anymore what those numbers say. Who better to transform you into the person you were created to be, than the One which created you? I used to have a very specific goal in mind and I would obsess over that number. I would weigh myself several times throughout the day. If I was down a pound, I would be happy. If I was up, I was miserable and depressed. I would manipulate the scale to work in my favor. For instance, I would weigh myself before a meal, naked, standing on one foot. It was an exhausting cycle and I became a slave to my scale.

Are they feeling a little snug or do they flow easily? Reflect on the portion sizes that you've been eating. Have you been adding a little extra food here and there or have you not eaten enough to stay in balance? Be honest with yourself. Once you take an inventory for that week, spend a few moments in quiet meditation and integrate what you have just learned. Choose to be willing to create the space to make any changes and act on them right away. If you are receptive, you will also be guided to your ideal body weight.

If the idea of not weighing yourself is a foreign concept to you, it may seem impossible at this time. A good way to start, especially if you weigh yourself every day, is to commit to weighing yourself once a week. You will soon begin to trust the process and your body. You can eventually expand that idea and get on the scale once a month. For example, you could choose one day out of the month, such as the 1st or the 15th, and commit to weigh yourself on that day. You will discover freedom from the scale. Eventually, you may want to give it up forever.

There is an exception to this rule since there are times when weighing yourself is a good idea. For instance, weighing yourself works when you are in denial. If you don't want to know how much you really weigh, then you should find out the truth. Weigh yourself if you have lost all concept of reality with your body. Do you still see your body as thin and trim even when you consume large amounts of food? Do you blame the dryer for shrinking your clothes if you have to buy

Reflections On

PRINCIPLE EIGHT

(The following reflections are offered to you as meditations that will help you nurture and cultivate a deeper connection with your silent voice within. While sitting quietly and breathing slowly and deeply, place your intention on one reflection at a time. Gently clear away thoughts of judgment and attachment, making room for the full mystery and sacredness of the message to permeate your heart and soul.)

~ I bless my balanced health because I know
it is divinely inspired.

~ I am grateful for my food and all the blessings
in my life.

~ I invite input from my innermost wisdom
regarding what I need to eat for optimal energy.

~ I dine with my honored guest because I
know I never have to face my challenges alone.

~ I trust that my every need is already satisfied.
I only need to claim it.

F. Which method would be most helpful to you: weighing yourself once-a-week, weighing yourself once-a-month or not weighing yourself at all? Why did you choose that answer?

G. If you do not wish to weigh yourself, list five inventory checks that will help keep your body in balanced health.

the statement, "I'm feeling angry". Are you really saying that you feel annoyed? Irritated? Sore? Enraged? Infuriated? Incensed? Bitter? Hostile? Perhaps all of these emotions apply to your anger. These eight different words relate to anger; but they each express a different degree of the feeling. There is plenty of room for misinterpretation.

Identifying and expressing your feelings is one of the first steps towards healing your emotions. If you don't identify the emotion that you're feeling, it is more challenging to work through it. One technique I use to unveil my feelings is to use an *analogy exercise*. Initially, I was afraid when I tried this technique because I spent my entire life running away from my feelings. I did a great job of stuffing them down with food. I was being taught to unmask them and I was terrified.

The core of this *analogy exercise* is to describe your feelings using different methods, such as: color, intensity, texture, sound, physical sensation, an image from nature, an animal, music, a song, or a mental picture. It is an extremely powerful tool when trying to get in touch with your true feelings. By the time you complete this exercise, you should know how you feel. This will make it easier for you to express yourself.

Here are two examples that I have used in the past. Notice how easy it is for you to identify and understand my feelings. When you express your feelings to others as an analogy, you can help them get a clearer and more accurate picture of your feelings.

Example 1: I feel like a scared cat, complete with a hunched-up back and hair that is standing straight up.

Once you choose your feeling, then describe it nine different ways.

Example 1: I feel "optimistic".

Example 2: I feel "enraged".

Express your feeling using a <u>color</u>:

Example 1: I feel optimistic like a rainbow of bright and beautiful colors.

Example 2: I feel enraged like the bright red flames shooting out of a burning building.

Express your feeling using a <u>level of intensity</u>: (1-to-10, with 10 being the most intense)

Example 1: The intensity of my feelings of optimism is an 8.

Example 2: The intensity of my enraged feelings is a 10.

Express your feeling by using a <u>texture</u>:

Example 1: I feel optimistic like a new crisp cotton shirt.

Example 2: I feel enraged like a bumpy, bulging blister that is ready to explode.

Express your feeling by using a <u>mental picture</u>:

*Example 1: I feel optimistic like a child making a wish, while blowing out the candles
on her birthday cake.*

Example 2: I feel enraged like a boxer in a prize fight.

Express your feeling by using <u>music or a song</u>:

Example 1: I feel optimistic like I would during the singing of the National Anthem.

Example 2: I feel enraged like the lyrics of a rap song on a classical radio station.

Once you have described your feelings by expressing them through the nine methods, you will have an accurate and clear idea of how to identify feelings. Understanding your feelings and being able to describe them is helpful to you. It is a valuable tool to help you share your feelings with others.

Learning how to describe and identify your feelings may seem scary and unfamiliar at first, but it gets easier with practice. Persevere through the uncomfortable stage and the resistance you have about identifying your feelings. If you are persistent, the reward will be worth the effort.

It may or may not be easy to pinpoint why you are feeling angry. Look inward for help if you cannot determine the cause. It may be something that occurred recently or it may be a trigger from something that happened in your childhood. You may be angry at someone and can't figure out why. Sometimes, they remind you of someone else and that will trigger a response.

An example is a time when I noticed that I was distancing myself from an old friend. For some reason, I just couldn't be around her anymore. She was a sweet, lovable woman, so I couldn't understand why I was feeling the resistance. There was no visible sign of discord or dissension. Nothing negative had happened that would cause my reaction. We would try to spend time together, but I would never follow through and cancel at the last minute. Almost a year went by and it was really beginning to bother me. It was causing tension in our relationship since we had not seen each other in a long time.

After trying to figure it out on my own, I knew that I needed to search inward and ask that light be shed on the issue. As I sat quietly I asked the question, "Why am I harboring feelings of anger towards this person?" I was persistent in asking that question and finally when I was ready to hear the answer, it came to me loud and clear.

I was angry with her because she was naturally thin and could eat whatever she wanted. Whenever the two of us were around food, she was able to eat the goodies that I could not eat. "Why can't I eat anything I want, like she can?" I would toward food and was able to learn and become inspired by them. What began as a challenge ended up being an amazing learning experience for me. It opened up a whole new level of commitment and interest in creating balanced health.

Learning about my anger also forced me to look at how judgmental I was. I hadn't realized how I was judging others in order to make myself feel better. I was trying hard to build bridges, but I was actually creating brick walls. This inspired me to commit to try to not judge people, situations or things. I'm not always perfect, but I have discovered that when I practice non-judgment, there is no anger or resentment as a result.

The reasons for your feelings of anger may not be revealed, but with guidance and by using the *analogy exercise*, you can move closer to unveiling the truth. By examining your feelings using all nine methods of description, you allow the gift of freedom and release. The more you turn it over to your infinite power, the easier it becomes and the quicker you will receive answers. The wave of difficult feelings will eventually pass if you choose not to hold on to them. You can let them go by choosing to deal with them.

DISTRESS AND FATIGUE:

It's important that you monitor your emotions closely, so you avoid the feelings of distress and fatigue. When you are feeling stressed or tired, you might make irrational decisions. Before you know it, you could be eating things you don't want

Fatigue is also a feeling that can upset the balance in your life. Even though it isn't always possible, try to get a full night's sleep. Getting the required amount of sleep is necessary for a healthy lifestyle. It's easy to stay up late watching television, working on a project, finishing up chores, or whatever you are doing at the time; but, try to resist the temptation. The world can look amazingly different when you are rested. Issues don't seem to affect you as much. You are better able to handle the day-to-day challenges with relative ease.

LONELINESS:

Feelings of loneliness can seem overwhelming at times. You may fill your days with lots of activities or work long hours in order to avoid the feelings. But somehow, someway, they will always surface.

I used to feel lonely and separated from the rest of the world. I desperately searched for a place to fit in. I felt different and distant because I was fat and filled with shame. I hid so many secrets, that I couldn't allow anyone to get close enough to see the "real me". I could be in a crowded room, yet still be lonely.

Here are some examples of ways to describe lonely feelings:

I feel lonely like a child who comes home from school to an empty house.

I feel lonely like I just lost my spouse or best friend.

night. This was a destructive behavior and it had a grave effect on me. I was gaining weight and my health was beginning to suffer. I wasn't able to get a decent night's sleep because I was stuffed with junk food. Then, I would wake up feeling horrible, as if I had a hangover. I still felt the lonely feelings, but now they were compounded with the feelings of shame and guilt that always accompanied a binge-eating episode. Again, I felt like a failure.

I knew I needed help in facing this challenge of sneaking food, since my best efforts to stop the behavior were failing. When I looked inward, I always found love and compassion. Sitting in the quietude of my soul, I would ask, "Why am I eating large quantities of food every time my husband leaves? What feelings am I trying to avoid?"

Soon, it was revealed to me that I was desperately trying to hide my feelings of loneliness, as well as my feelings of fear that he wouldn't be coming back. The excess food was the result of me trying to run away from those feelings. I clung to the food as a false source of security and reassurance that I would never be alone.

The *analogy exercise* helped me get in touch with my deepest feelings of loneliness in regard to this issue. I wrote in my journal, *"My lonely feelings can be described like my heart being ripped out of my body and it is aching to reconnect with me."*

Once I was able to get clear about the intensity of my feelings of loneliness, I was then able to share them with my husband. I found great relief being able to express my true feelings of deprivation come from, try to get an accurate description of them. This should help you to fully understand the depths of your feelings.

The *analogy exercise* is helpful when describing feelings of deprivation because it will prompt you to examine the intensity of your feelings. Keep going deeper and ask yourself, "Why am I feeling deprived? What is making me feel deprived? Am I letting someone else cause me to feel deprived?" These questions require spiritual insight and patience as you explore your deprived feelings.

Here are some examples of descriptions of deprived feelings:

> *I feel deprived like being the only child out of six children in my family that didn't receive presents from Santa Claus.*

> *I feel deprived like an infant whose mother has passed away.*

> *I feel deprived like a woman who desperately wants a child, yet she can't get pregnant, and her biological clock is ticking.*

> *I feel deprived like a homeless person on the street and I don't have any shoes.*

> *My intensity of feeling deprived is a 9 (on a scale of 1-to-10).*

Deprived feelings can often seem like hunger. Read your body carefully. It may be telling you that it is dealing with unsettled feelings that you have tried to stuff with food. You

Reflections On

PRINCIPLE NINE

(The following reflections are offered to you as meditations that will help you nurture and cultivate a deeper connection with your silent voice within. While sitting quietly and breathing slowly and deeply, place your intention on one reflection at a time. Gently clear away thoughts of judgment and attachment, making room for the full mystery and sacredness of the message to permeate your heart and soul.)

- ~ My best intentions can disappear if I allow difficult or unpleasant feelings to overcome me.
- ~ By examining my feelings using all nine methods in the *analogy exercise*, I give myself the gift of freedom and release.
- ~ I am committed to uncovering the root of my discord as quickly as possible.
- ~ I am committed to be free of judgment about people, situations, or things that happen.
- ~ A healthy lifestyle requires that I get the necessary amount of sleep for my body.
- ~ I stick to a routine and eat at scheduled times every day.

PRINCIPLE TEN

Build Up Your Spiritual Chain of Support

"Become willing to see the hand of God and accept it as a friend's offer to help you with what you are doing."
- Julia Cameron

When you are ready to practice this new balanced lifestyle, enlist the help of a trusted friend, family member, spiritual advisor, psychologist, therapist, counselor, health practitioner, personal coach or join a support group. Find someone who can share in your joys and accomplishments and will support you in any frustrations and anxiety that you have to face. Seek out people who inspire you to keep reaching for new heights and can be compassionate and understanding as you walk forward. Having spiritual support is very helpful during your journey to balanced health.

For many of you, the concept of reaching out to someone will seem daunting and difficult. This could be because you

They are present to help you realize your own strength and help you discover how to help yourself.

They are present to love you, just the way you are.

One way to encourage communication and openness with someone in your support system is for the both of you to read this book together. Each time you visit, you can share one or two paragraphs and then discuss your thoughts and feelings. You may also choose to share answers from the Gifts of Awareness section. Eventually, you will have worked your way through the book and a bond will have been created. At the end of the book, I have included a page entitled, *The Ties That Bind Us*. It is intended to establish your foundation and purpose for gathering with your buddy. I suggest that every time you get together, one of you reads this page out loud to the other.

Support groups that focus on eating behaviors may also be a valuable resource. There are several based on the 12-Step program and they can offer fellowship and a sense of community.

Another way to build your support system is by attending a retreat or workshop. A bond forms when participants share their thoughts and feelings in a group setting. This is due in part to the fact they are all walking similar journeys and have a common goal or interest.

If you feel the need for professional assistance, seek out a psychologist, therapist, or counselor who specializes in personal success coaching, workshops or support groups based on a spiritual solution to weight loss and balanced health, please contact me at www.BronwynMarmo.com.

Whether you choose any or all of the available support systems that have been mentioned, it's important to remember that these are only a means to the end. They are not the goal. The final authority is your silent voice. It's important to focus and discern the direction of your innermost wisdom, always remembering that this is your ultimate authority. Look within for guidance and follow your soul.

Gifts of Awareness

PRINCIPLE TEN

(Gifts of Awareness are special questions that will help you unveil the presence of divinity in your life. Answer these questions in a personal journal and at your own pace. They are pearls of wisdom and discovery that are revealed during the process of transformation. They are available to you as a guide along your journey. During this time, practice being loving and gentle with yourself. By being tolerant and accepting toward yourself and others, you create the space for change.)

A. Describe your relationship with your innermost truth.

B. Are you relying on the guidance you receive?
   If not, why are you resistant? Are you resistant to listening or to following the guidance?

C. Are there two people currently in your life that can support you as you grow and change? (They may be a trusted friend, family member, spiritual advisor, psychologist, therapist, counselor, support group or personal success coach.)

D. What special qualities do these two people have?

E. Do you think a support group may be helpful to you at this time?

ᏒᏒ PRINCIPLE ELEVEN ᏒᏒ

Share Your Love

*"When we truly care for ourselves, it becomes possible to care
far more profoundly about other people.
The more alert and sensitive we are to our own needs,
the more loving and generous we can be toward others."*
- Eda LeShan

It is important to keep the flow of love circulating. You will have an abundance of love showered upon you as you create the support group discussed in Principle 10. You pass it on by sharing it with others.

Giving and receiving are part of the same circle. Share the love that is in you and around you. Share the joy that has been brought into your life. Share the wisdom that you have learned as you have been walking your journey.

Blessings are intended to be shared. In this way, they divide and multiply. You cannot give away "all" your love.

a shield. The extra padding prevented me from getting too close to him or letting him get close to me.

I couldn't escape the maternal longing and I realized that I must go see my son. Once I made the decision, it felt like I was being swept down a river and couldn't stop, even if I had wanted to. There was a burning desire for me to see him that seemed much bigger than I was. His adoptive parents encouraged the visit and invited me to stay in their home on the weekend of the visit. I took a huge leap of faith and stepped into the unknown. My steadfast belief in my innermost strength would provide me with the courage to see it through. Even though I had faith in my guide, I was extremely scared.

When I arrived at his home, I found him playing in the front yard. I immediately dropped to my knees in front of him to get a closer look. His angelic beauty struck me when the late afternoon sun beamed across his back and projected a halo of light all around him. I gazed into his crystal blue eyes. They looked almost translucent and offered me a window into his soul. As we continued to stare at each other, I knew a deep connection had been made - a connection so strong that only he and I would remember it after such a long separation.

I held my son close to me and wrapped my arms around him. It seemed very natural and familiar as I stroked his golden blonde hair and brushed my lips against his soft cheeks. His features were very delicate and he still had the same sweet smell that he had as a newborn. It seemed as if not one day had gone by since we had parted. I couldn't stop staring at

After giving myself the gift of a visit to my first child, I knew that my womb was healed. I also knew that my life was changed forever. Comfort and peace surrounded me as I realized that my son was exactly where he needed to be and with the family that was perfect for him. I returned home with an increased awareness of love and appreciation for my husband and my other two children. I realized that I had connected so much pain to my first son's birth, but that I then transferred the pain to them.

The trip helped break the cycle of destruction in my marriage. By grace, we were able to rekindle a relationship that felt like when we were dating. I learned many lessons from the little boy I physically gave away. He showed me the other side of love – one that doesn't hurt and can be shared freely. This side is never controlled or manipulated. This side may not make sense on the surface, yet it makes perfect sense when you look at the bigger picture. This perfect child taught me that pure love is a complete abandonment of ego. It is being present in the moment so that you can give and receive love with a full and open heart.

This lesson also altered my relationship with my other children as well. Because of the heart-breaking experience of my first birth, I had never totally embraced motherhood. I realized that I was missing a huge part of my life because I was not freely sharing my love. Not only was I missing out on the present moments of my life, but I was also missing out on the gifts of their life. The feeling of pain has been washed being available to others and seeking only the highest and best for them.

Make giving a regular part of your life. Reach out and help others. You will discover that when you turn your focus away from yourself and away from food, you will have an abundance of compassion, strength, courage and love to give away. There is a great healing around the issue of food when you give away food and other "excesses" in your life. You can volunteer by serving meals to the homeless, sponsor a hungry child, or give to your local food pantry. The more you divide and multiply the blessings in your life, the more you will receive.

Give even if you think you don't have anything to offer. When you are being of service to another, the areas where you think you are lacking can be filled in. When you live your life as an example of infinite love, you will find ways to love that will amaze you. Love your enemies and love those that you think are the most difficult to love. By creating love and living in a constant state of being "in love" with life, then love lives in you.

A beautiful example of Principle Eleven is the life of St. Francis of Assisi, lover of all creation and Patron Saint of animals and the environment. He was constantly celebrating his life and found many different ways to give praise. He would bless even the smallest things. The well-known prayer by St. Francis has amazing power and brings the gift of healing. I make it an integral part of my meditation time. I began to

Reflections On

PRINCIPLE ELEVEN

(The following reflections are offered to you as meditations that will help you nurture and cultivate a deeper connection with your silent voice within. While sitting quietly and breathing slowly and deeply, place your intention on one reflection at a time. Gently clear away thoughts of judgment and attachment, making room for the full mystery and sacredness of the message to permeate your heart and soul.)

- ~ Because giving and receiving are all the same, I share the love that I receive.
- ~ Blessings are intended to be shared – when I share them, they will divide and multiply.
- ~ When I love others freely, I am abundantly supplied with more than I can ever give away.
- ~ I am constantly being "filled-up" by a never-ending well of love.
- ~ I reach out and help others in order to turn my focus away from myself and food. I am given an abundance of compassion, strength, courage and love as I do this.
- ~ I give even when I think I have nothing to offer.
- ~ When I meditate on the Prayer of St. Francis and weave the principles into my life, I see dramatic changes in my world.

PRINCIPLE TWELVE

Know You Are Blessed Beyond Belief

"I don't believe, I know."
- Carl Jung

Insanity
By Bronwyn Marmo
June 3, 1997

"Insanity is being so full, yet I continue to stuff my face.
Insanity is gaining lots of weight and not being able to stop.
Insanity is starting a diet in the morning, then by 10 a.m.
stuffing a chocolate-chip cookie in my mouth.
Insanity is feeling so out of control.
Insanity is driving to the store in the middle of the night for food.
Insanity is eating a whole box of donuts
in the car before getting home, then eating a big dinner.
Insanity is the shame and guilt I feel whenever I binge.

trusted guide. Every time you look in the mirror, you will see divinity looking back at you. Every time you feel downhearted because you may have overeaten or not eaten correctly, you get to bask in the loving light that is filled with abundant mercy, compassion, comfort and strength. Your power source is within you and around you at all times. Begin to overcome your health challenges by acknowledging and nurturing this intimate relationship. What a gift it is to be constantly reminded that you are complete.

I've come to realize that I am blessed beyond belief as a result of the hardships I have endured. My challenges have been based on food, body image and self-esteem. Your challenges may be the same or different. Whatever they are, consider yourself blessed. Now, I say, "Thank You, for my food challenges. Thank You, for providing me with this constant reminder that You are with me every step of the way. Thank You, for drawing me nearer to You every day. Thank You, for loving me so much that You gave me life."

I used to pray with great anguish that God would remove my obsession with food, my body and my weight. I was so tired of fixating on them. I just wanted my challenges to disappear so that I never had to think about them again. I wanted to be free to go about my day in peace and serenity.

As you now know, my prayers were answered, but in a manner that far exceeded my expectations. They were answered in a way that left me feeling empowered, with my self-respect and dignity intact. The self-defeating thoughts

Reflections On

PRINCIPLE TWELVE

(The following reflections are offered to you as meditations that will help you nurture and cultivate a deeper connection with your silent voice within. While sitting quietly and breathing slowly and deeply, place your intention on one reflection at a time. Gently clear away thoughts of judgment and attachment, making room for the full mystery and sacredness of the message to permeate your heart and soul.)

~ I know that I am blessed beyond belief.

~ As I search for peace with my food, weight, body image and self-esteem, I am handed many opportunities to reflect inward.

~ When I acknowledge and nurture an intimate relationship with my innermost truth, I will overcome my challenges.

~ I am constantly reminded that I am complete.

~ All prayers are answered; not necessarily in the way I expect, but always for my highest and best good.

~ My self-defeating thoughts still arise occasionally, but now I can choose how I am going to respond to those thoughts.

~ I am watching the wonders and miracles unfold before my eyes.

AFTERWORD

Living the Life You've Always Dreamed

"The world is round and the place which may seem like the end may also be only the beginning."
- Ivy Baker Priest

I hope and pray that this book gives you the comfort, strength, determination and inspiration you need to walk your journey and create a healthier and balanced life.

Never lose sight of the big picture; that you are loved more than you can ever imagine. It's because you are loved that you are going to continue your transformation. You will be gently nudged to make positive changes in your life as you are being molded and shaped into the person you are destined to become.

There are many empowering thoughts and ideas in this book that will help you achieve your goal of balanced health. Yet, you might be asking yourself, "Where do I begin?" Well,

As you begin your journey to balanced health, may you rely on your truth and know that the answers lie within you. You do have the power to choose!
With love and admiration,

Bronwyn

or attachment. Then, ever-so-gently, bring ourselves
back to our innermost truth.

5. We develop an inner acceptance that is always saying,
   "Yes". "Yes" to our innermost truth. "Yes" to love. "Yes"
   to balanced health. "Yes" to life. We know the highest
   and best "Yes" is always being said to us.

6. We allow ourselves the gift of imperfection and embrace
   our own humanness. It's okay if we are not perfect.

This is a safe and secure place. We know that when we
share our innermost thoughts and feelings, that they will not
be repeated or discussed outside this room.

Are we in agreement?

We are bound together like family.

To all of us, welcome home.

Caddy, Eileen. *Opening Doors Within*. Forres, Scotland: The Findhorn Press, 1987.

Cameron, Julia. *The Artist's Way: A Spiritual Path to Higher Creativity*. New York: Jeremy P. Tarcher/Perigee Books/Putnam Publishing Group, 1992.

Campbell, Joseph. *The Power of Myth*, with Bill Moyers. New York: Anchor Books, A Division of Random House, Inc., 1988.

Colwin, Laurie. *Home Cooking: A Writer in the Kitchen*. New York: Alfred A. Knopf, 1988.
----. *More Home Cooking: A Writer Returns to the Kitchen*. New York: Harper Collins, 1993.

Ferguson, Sheila. *Soul Food: Classic Cuisine from the Deep South*. London and New York: Weidenfeld & Nicolson, 1989.

Holmes, Marjorie. *I've Got to Talk to Somebody, God*. New York: Doubleday. 1968.

Johnson, Samuel. *Samuel Johnson, Oxford Authors*, edited by D. Greene. Oxford/ New York: Oxford University Press, 1984.

Keating, Thomas. *Invitation to Love: The Way of Christian Contemplation*. New York: The Continuum Publishing Company, 1992.
----. *Open Mind, Open Heart: The Contemplative Dimension of the Gospel*. New York: The Continuum Publishing Company, 1986.

GLOSSARY OF NAMES

This glossary was originally created because of my desire to learn more about the lives of those authors who wrote such incredible words of inspiration. I am grateful to each one of them because their writing has given me strength, encouragement and hope. I hope you find the background information interesting. If you wish to find out more about a particular author, perhaps this information will assist you in your search.

Anne De Lenclos (1615-1705) was a French author and patron of the arts.

Anne Lamott has written several best-selling, non-fiction books and six novels. She is a past recipient of a Guggenheim Fellowship, and has taught at UC Davis. Her column in Salon magazine was voted Best of the Web by Newsweek. She currently lives in Northern California.

Anne Wilson Schaef, PhD, is a best-selling author, lecturer, organizational consultant, former psychotherapist, and workshop leader. She trains health care professionals throughout the world in Living Process Facilitation. She lives in Boulder, Colorado.

Baba Hari Dass (1923-) was born in India. The monk and Master Yogi was classically trained in traditional Ashtanga Yoga. He has maintained a continual vow of silence since

Tibetans, who believe him to be the 14th earthly incarnation of the heavenly deity of compassion and mercy. In 1989, he received the Nobel Peace Prize Laureate. He is said to be bridging the gap between traditional Eastern wisdom and modern Western psychology.

Eckhart Tolle (1948-) is said to be one of the most original and inspiring spiritual teachers of our time. At the core of his teachings lies the transformation of individual and collective human consciousness - a global spiritual awakening.

Eda LeShan (1922-2002) was the author of more than 30 books for adults and children. She was also a counselor, educator, and playwright.

Eileen Caddy (1917-) is said to be one of the foremost spiritual teachers of our times. She is the co-founder of Findhorn, an international spiritual community in Scotland. She says she sees her role as helping others turn within and find their own inner direction.

Eknath Easwaran (1910-1999) was respected around the world as one of the twentieth century's great spiritual teachers. He is known for his ability to bring spiritual ideals into everyday life. He founded the Blue Mountain Center of Meditation in Berkeley, California.

Eleanor Roosevelt (1884-1962) is said to be one of the 20th century's most influential and admired women. Her humanitarian efforts on behalf of children, the oppressed and the poor earned her the title "First Lady of the World." Her hus-

Jalaluddin Rumi (1207-1273) is one of the great spiritual masters and poetic geniuses. He was the founder of the Mawlawi Sufi order, a leading mystical brotherhood of Islam. The name Mowlana Jalaluddin Rumi stands for love and ecstatic flight into the infinite.

Jean Anthelme Brillat-Savarin (1775-1826) was a French lawyer, magistrate, and politician. He wrote one of the most celebrated works on food, *The Physiology of Taste*. This was published only months before his death.

Johann Wolfgang von Goethe (1749-1832) was a German poet, novelist, playwright, courtier, and natural philosopher. He was one of the greatest figures in Western literature.

John Ruskin (1819-1900) was one of the greatest figures of the Victorian age. He was a poet, artist, critic, social revolutionary and conservationist.

Joseph Campbell (1904-1987) was an American writer who is said to be one of the world's foremost scholars of mythology and comparative religion. Campbell's theories were made popular with the Public Broadcasting System series of television interviews with Bill Moyers. The PBS interviews were published as a book, which became a bestseller.

Joseph Murphy (1898-1981) was a Minister-Director of the Church of Divine Science in Los Angeles for 28 years. He spent a good part of his life studying Eastern religions, and was a scholar of the I-Ching. This is a Chinese book of divination whose origins are lost in history.

Ludwig Mies van der Rohe (1886-1969) was a German-born, American Architect. He ranks as one of the most notable architects of the 20th century. He created buildings that provided a new style, one that reshaped architecture following World War II.

Mahatma Gandhi (1869-1948) was an Indian spiritual and political leader and humanitarian. He became one of the most respected spiritual and political leaders of the 1900's. Gandhi helped free the Indian people from British rule through non-violent resistance, and is honored by his people as the father of the Indian Nation.

Marjorie Holmes (1910-2002) was an award-winning American author, columnist and teacher. Her books, which have sold in the millions, bring biblical days to life. She attributed her success to her ability to make the Holy Family as real as the folks next door.

Martha Graham (1894-1991) was a dancer and choreographer, as well as, the central figure of the modern dance movement. In more than 180 works created during a career of over fifty years, Graham developed an original technique involving the expression of primal emotions through stylized bodily movement of great intensity.

Mary Antin (1881-1949) was born in Russia. At the age of 13, she immigrated to the United States with her family. She wrote a moving and eloquent record of her experience in her autobiography *The Promised Land*, published in 1912. It was

Nikos Kazantzakis (1883-1957) was one of the most important Greek writers, poets and philosophers of the 20th century.

Oscar Wilde (1854-1900) was an Irish dramatist, novelist and poet.

Paule Marshall (1929-) is an African-American author and educator. She was born and raised in Brooklyn, New York. She is a Professor of English at Virginia Commonwealth University in Richmond, Virginia.

Rebecca West (1892-1983) was an English journalist, novelist, and critic. She was born in London, England of Scottish-Irish parentage. West is perhaps best-known for her reports on the Nuremberg trials of 1945-46. In 1954, she was described as "the best journalist alive".

Reinhold Niebuhr (1892-1971) was a theologian, teacher, and social philosopher. He has invoked the ancient insights of Christianity to illuminate the experience and fortify the will of the modern age. The origin of the Serenity Prayer is not exactly known, yet is commonly attributed to Niebuhr. It was adapted by the founders of Alcoholics Anonymous as a centerpiece of the various 12-step programs.

Richard Rohr (1943-) is a Franciscan priest of the New Mexico Province. He founded the Center for Action and Contemplation in Albuquerque, New Mexico in 1986. He has written numerous books and gives retreats and lectures internationally.

Thich Nhat Hanh (1926-) is a Vietnamese Buddhist monk, poet, peace activist, and the author of more than 75 books of prose, poetry and prayers. He lives in exile in a small monastic community in France where he teaches, writes, gardens, and works to help refugees worldwide. He conducts retreats throughout the world on the art of "mindful living".

Thomas Keating is a Cistercian priest, monk, and abbot. He is a co-founder of the Centering Prayer Movement and of Contemplative Outreach. He presents the Centering Prayer method and its related mystical theology to gatherings of non-Christians, Protestants, and Roman Catholics worldwide. He currently lives at St. Benedict's Monastery in Snowmass, Colorado.

Thomas Merton (1915-1968) was an American writer and Trappist monk at Our Lady of Gethsemani Abbey in Trappist, Kentucky. He authored more than 70 books that include poetry, personal journals, collections of letters, social criticism and writings on peace, social justice and ecumenicism.

Ursula K. LeGuin (1929-) is an American author of science fiction, fantasy, and children's stories. She has published over 100 short stories collected in eight volumes; three collections of essays; 13 books for children; five volumes of poetry; and 19 novels. She has received many awards for her works, including the Boston Globe-Hornbook Award for juvenile fiction.

William Hazlitt (1778-1830) was an English essayist. He was one of the great masters of the miscellaneous essay, said to display a keen intellect, sensibility, and wide scope of interest and knowledge.

Radical Grace: Daily Meditations by Richard Rohr, Edited by John Bookser Feister. Copyright © 1995 by Richard Rohr and John Bookser Feister. Used by permission of St. Anthony Messenger Press.

Practicing The Power of Now by Eckhart Tolle. Copyright © 1999 by Eckhart Tolle. Used by permission of New World Library. www.newworldlibrary.com/800-972-6657

Selected quote by Mary Lou Cook. Copyright © by Mary Lou Cook. Permission personally granted by Mary Lou Cook.

Simple Abundance: A Daybook of Comfort and Joy by Sarah Ban Breathnach. Copyright © 1995 by Sarah Ban Breathnach. Quote by Melinda Burns used by permission of Warner Books. Permission also personally granted by Melinda Burns.

New Seeds of Contemplation by Thomas Merton. Copyright © 1961 by The Abbey of Gethsemani, Inc. Reprinted by permission of New Directions Publishing Corp.

Opening Doors Within by Eileen Caddy. Copyright © 1986 by Eileen Caddy. Used by permission of Findhorn Press.

story. It helps you read the signs of our times – the waist line."
Fr. Carl J. Arico, Contemplative Outreach of New Jersey and Author of A Taste of Silence: A Guide to the Fundamentals of Centering Prayer

"Bronwyn has done a beautiful job of breaking the healing journey into gifts of awareness that will benefit many. She ably leads the way. The description of her awakening is its own power. You will not be disappointed."
Paula D'Arcy, Author of Gift of the Red Bird

"I have been so fortunate to work one-on-one with Bronwyn and discover new and realistic ways of setting myself up for success and faith, instead of fear and disappointment."
Patricia Kelly, Personal Coaching Client

"I have struggled with weight and body image issues my entire life. Bronwyn's spiritual approach to balanced health has given me the key to a door I thought was locked forever."
Lisa Simkins, Personal Coaching Client

"Bronwyn's approach to weight loss doesn't come in pre-packaged foods, selected menus, or exercise guides... it comes from within. Her presence exudes such great compassion and understanding. I will never look at weight-loss in the same way again. My true journey has begun."
Ruth Ann Lopez, Workshop Participant

I Would Love To Hear From You!

If you have any questions or comments concerning the
contents of this book, or if you would like information about
workshops, retreats, or personal coaching,
please contact me:

Bronwyn Marmo
Phone: (480) 314-3333
E-mail: Bronwyn@BronwynMarmo.com
Website: www.BronwynMarmo.com

Or Write to:
Bronwyn Marmo
c/o Triple B Publishing
11445 E. Via Linda, Suite 2 - 249
Scottsdale, AZ 85259

QUICK ORDER FORM

Yes! I would like to order copies of this book for my friends.

Telephone Orders: (480) 314-3333 Have your credit card ready.

Fax Orders: (480) 452-0588

E-mail Orders: Orders@BronwynMarmo.com

Online Orders: www.BronwynMarmo.com
This is a secure site.

Mail Orders: Please send checks payable to:

Triple B Publishing, 11445 E. Via Linda, Suite 2-249, Scottsdale, AZ 85259

Please send me _____ copies of this book at the price of $19.95 U.S. per book (Higher in other countries). I understand that I may return any item for a full refund. No questions asked.

U.S. Shipping and Handling: Please add $5.50 for first book and $3.00 for each additional book.

International Shipping and Handling: Please add $11.00 for first book and $6.00 for each additional book.

Sales Tax: Please add 7.7% for books shipped to an Arizona address.

Total Amount of Sale:_____.

Name:_____

Address:_____

City:_____State:_____Zip:_____

Telephone:_____E-mail Address:_____

Payment: Please circle method of payment below.

Check   Credit Card: Visa   MasterCard

Card number:_____

Name on Card:_____

Expiration Date:_____

Signature of Card Holder:_____

QUICK ORDER FORM

Yes! I would like to order copies of this book for my friends.

Telephone Orders: (480) 314-3333 Have your credit card ready.

Fax Orders: (480) 452-0588

E-mail Orders: Orders@BronwynMarmo.com

Online Orders: www.BronwynMarmo.com
This is a secure site.

Mail Orders: Please send checks payable to:

Triple B Publishing, 11445 E. Via Linda, Suite 2-249, Scottsdale, AZ 85259

Please send me _____ copies of this book at the price of $19.95 U.S. per book (Higher in other countries). I understand that I may return any item for a full refund. No questions asked.

U.S. Shipping and Handling: Please add $5.50 for first book and $3.00 for each additional book.

International Shipping and Handling: Please add $11.00 for first book and $6.00 for each additional book.

Sales Tax: Please add 7.7% for books shipped to an Arizona address.

Total Amount of Sale:_____.

Name:_____

Address:_____

City:_____State:_____Zip:_____

Telephone:_____E-mail Address:_____

Payment: Please circle method of payment below.

Check   Credit Card: Visa   MasterCard

Card number:_____

Name on Card:_____

Expiration Date:_____

Signature of Card Holder:_____

Yes! I would like to order copies of this book for my friends.

Telephone Orders: (480) 314-3333 Have your credit card ready.

Fax Orders: (480) 452-0588

E-mail Orders: Orders@BronwynMarmo.com

Online Orders: www.BronwynMarmo.com

This is a secure site.

Mail Orders: Please send checks payable to:

Triple B Publishing, 11445 E. Via Linda, Suite 2-249, Scottsdale, AZ 85259

Please send me _____ copies of this book at the price of $19.95 U.S. per book (Higher in other countries). I understand that I may return any item for a full refund. No questions asked.

U.S. Shipping and Handling: Please add $5.50 for first book and $3.00 for each additional book.

International Shipping and Handling: Please add $11.00 for first book and $6.00 for each additional book.

Sales Tax: Please add 7.7% for books shipped to an Arizona address.

Total Amount of Sale:_____.

Name:_____

Address:_____

City:_____State:_____Zip:_____

Telephone:_____E-mail Address:_____

Payment: Please circle method of payment below.

Check   Credit Card: Visa   MasterCard

Card number:_____

Name on Card:_____

Expiration Date:_____

Signature of Card Holder:_____